TURNING BOXES

WITH RICHARD RAFFAN

COMPLETELY REVISED AND UPDATED

The Taunton Press

Text © 2002 by Richard Raffan
Photographs © 2002 by Richard Raffan unless otherwise credited
Illustrations © 2002 by The Taunton Press, Inc.

The Taunton Press
Inspiration for hands-on living™

The Taunton Press, Inc., 63 South Main Street, PO Box 5506, Newtown, CT 06470-5506
e-mail: tp@taunton.com

Distributed by Publishers Group West

DESIGNER: Rosalind Wanke
LAYOUT ARTIST: Suzie Yannes
ILLUSTRATORS: Lisa Long, Michael Gellatly
COVER PHOTOGRAPHER: Richard Raffan assisted by Les Fortescue

LIBRARY OF CONGRESS CATALOGING-IN-PUBLICATION DATA:
Raffan, Richard.
    Turning boxes with Richard Raffan.– Completely rev. and updated.
        p. cm.
    Includes index.
    ISBN 1-56158-509-2
        1. Turning. 2. Wooden boxes. I. Title.

TT201 .R3378 2002
    684'.08–dc21

Printed in the United States of America
10 9 8 7 6 5 4 3 2 1

ABOUT YOUR SAFETY

Working with wood is inherently dangerous. Using hand or power tools improperly or ignoring safety practices can lead to permanent injury or even death. Don't try to perform operations you learn about here (or elsewhere) unless you're certain they are safe for you. If something about an operation doesn't feel right, don't do it. Look for another way. We want you to enjoy the craft, so please keep safety foremost in your mind whenever you're in the shop.

Co/
A05

TURNING BOXES

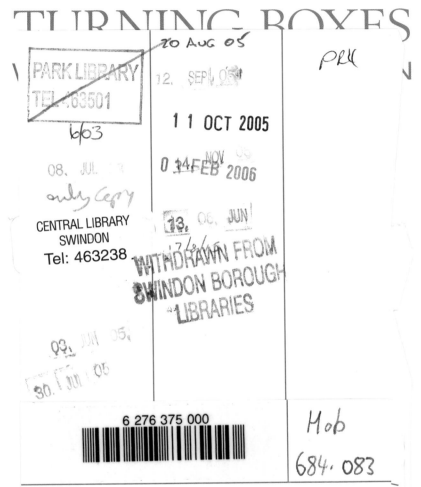

20 AUG 05

PARK LIBRARY
TEL 463501
6/03

12. SEP 05

PRU

11 OCT 2005

08. JUL

only copy

0 14FEB 2006
NOV 05

CENTRAL LIBRARY
SWINDON
Tel: 463238

13. 06. JUN

03. JUN 05

30. JUN 05

Mob
684· 083

Items should be returned to the library from which the
were borrowed by closing time on or before the da
stamped above, unless a renewal has been granted.

🌳 Swindon BOROUGH COUNCIL

SBC.LIB 02

Acknowledgments

Woodturning has been very good to me and taken me across the world to all manner of out-of-the-way places. It's put me in the way of interesting people from all walks of life whom I would not otherwise have had the chance to meet. And from them I've gained wonderful insights into not just woodturning but art, design, communication, and a mass of other bits and pieces that make life and the world so interesting. Thank you one and all.

Contents

Introduction

When I decided to turn wood for a living late in 1969, I knew nothing about the craft. But I did have it in mind to make boxes—especially little boxes—for rings, pills, and spices, or for the more personal treasures we each possess. I had no inkling then of how challenging this would be, or of the many thousands of boxes I was destined to make throughout the decades following. Even now, after 30 years, my fascination with this particular aspect of woodturning continues. Much of this has to do with the challenge of making a lid that fits just tightly enough that it comes off with a soft plop. Then there are the visual aspects concerned with proportions, the combining of curves and detailing, which in turn must relate to the tactile qualities experienced when the box is handled.

But above all, the attraction of boxes seems to lie in their enigmatic role as mini storehouses that might contain anything from a collection of tiny shells or ball bearings to a lover's eyelash or mummified frog. Most of us feel the need to hoard mementos of times past, which the casually curious might only guess at, and how better to do that than in a group of boxes on some shelf, clutched together as a sculptural form in their own right.

You can make special containers for specific objects or with hidden compartments. These boxes might not be commercially viable, but they are just the thing for any hobbyist—ideal personal gifts that also stand a good chance of becoming the heirlooms future generations will treasure. Boxes can be all manner of shapes and sizes and it is not mandatory that the internal form should reflect the exterior; box walls do not have to be thin and even. Thus there is scope for all manner of design solutions to surprise or taunt our expectations of how a piece should look or feel.

I have included a few technical hints to hone your skills, but I don't dwell on basic techniques since these are set down in detail in *Turning Wood with Richard Raffan* (The Taunton Press, 2001). Chapter 4 details how to turn a basic lidded end-grain box with an over-fitting lid. Most of the boxes in this book have lids that fit in the same manner: The inside and outside forms vary. If you are new to box turning, make a few simple forms using this chapter as a guide and strive for a nice, soft suction fit before you move on to more complicated pieces.

You can find inspiration for new forms just about everywhere, in seed pods and blossoms, finials on housing or many older public buildings in so many parts of the world, or old-style mailboxes and bollards. The Taj Mahal and the equally famous roofs of the Kremlin led me to explore similar forms for several years before a ceramic Japanese tea jar sent me off in another direction.

There are dozens of forms to set you on your own path of discovery and to help the development of your own style. Rather than copy them, let these be a springboard for your imagination, triggering some variation of your own.

Like most of the world, I use metric scales to measure. For those who don't, imperial measurements have been rounded to the nearest ⅛ in. for the sake of convenience. Accurate measuring in the projects is mostly achieved without rulers or tape measures, and I don't think the world will fall apart at my failure to measure to the nearest ¹⁄₃₂ in. the diameter of any piece illustrated.

1

EQUIPMENT & TOOLS

Having the right tools makes any task easier and more enjoyable. The good news is that for turning boxes you can get by with few tools because the scale of the work allows you to use small machines and the basic techniques don't require many turning tools. The growing interest in woodturning over the past 15 years and the desire of manufacturers to get a slice of the action mean that woodturners are now offered a mountain of choices pertaining to all aspects of turning. It's a tool junkie's dream world. You can get set up for box turning for relatively little money compared with other forms of turning or cabinetmaking, but you may have to sift through many widgets and less practical items to find wonderful tools at competitive prices.

What follows is a brief description of the basic equipment I use for turning boxes. Everything I describe is available commercially, so you should be able to find something similar to the description when you shop for your tools. If you already own turning equipment, there are pointers on how to tune your lathe and sharpen your turning tools.

Lathe

The lathe is the heart of your turning activity. You need a machine that will spin the wood without vibrating and a tool rest that is easy to adjust and solid enough to provide firm support for the tools.

Lathes come in all sizes, so if you are going to make bowls as well as boxes, you'll need a machine similar to the one in the top photo on the facing page, or, if you want to turn spindles, a long-bed version with sufficient space between centers to accept the lengths you have in mind. But if your interest is turning on a small scale, a mini lathe will be more than adequate and a quarter of the price (see the bottom photo on the facing page).

A tail center is not essential, so you can adapt an old headstock or even make one using a shaft mounted in bearings on a solid base. You should ensure that the spindle thread accepts a standard chuck by using a popular thread size: 1 in. by 8 (24mm by 3.5) and 1¼ in. by 8 (30mm by 3.5) are common. Good tool-rest assemblies can often be recycled from scrapped metalwork or metal spinning lathes or purchased as separate items from lathe manufacturers.

No matter which size you opt for and regardless of whether you buy a lathe or create your own, there are certain aspects of all lathes that you must consider. Here's a checklist.

• **The construction** Because lathes need to be solid and, ideally, vibration free, they should be constructed of cast iron, which goes clunk when you hit it, rather than steel or aluminum, which rings and is therefore vibrating. The best manufactured lathes have a cast-iron headstock, tailstock, and rest assembly on a cast-iron bed, although for the bed heavy wood beams can be substituted.

• **The stand** The stand must keep the lathe rock-steady, so it needs to be heavy or have a well-designed A-frame. Stands constructed of sheet steel should be 3/16 in. (5mm) thick or more, so that a good short-bed lathe on its stand should weigh around 400 lbs. (180kg). As a rule of thumb, if you can move the machine easily, it's too lightweight. If you have a lightweight stand, try bracing it with sheets of plywood or mounting it against a wall. A good alternative is to build a stand yourself from lumber and plywood or medium-density fiberboard (MDF), which absorbs vibration better than most materials. The stand in the drawing on p. 6 is simply screwed and glued together, but many turners take this concept and create their own variation with drawers or built-in dust collection.

• **The headstock** I recommend a drive shaft at least 1 in. (25mm) in diameter set in sealed ball or roller bearings. Smaller-diameter shafts never seem to have the strength to support a chuck and consequently vibrate and chatter. Avoid solid-bronze bearings: They have been responsible for some of my worst turning experiences, demanding constant and mostly futile adjustment. Another nice feature is a hollow shaft, which enables you to knock out a drive center or waste wood or even to set up a vacuum chuck. A drive-shaft lock is essential to facilitate easy mounting of blanks in most chucks.

The best lathes are cast iron and robust. This short-bed Vicmarc weighs around 400 lbs. (180kg). The black space behind the chuck is the dust-collection hood.

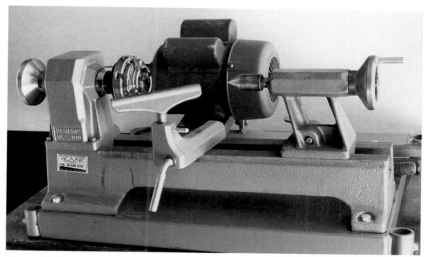

A mini lathe occupies very little space, but it still needs to be heavy to dampen vibration. This lathe weighs around 57 lbs. (26kg); with the base and motor added, it's 100 lbs. (45kg).

The lathe is the heart of your turning activity.

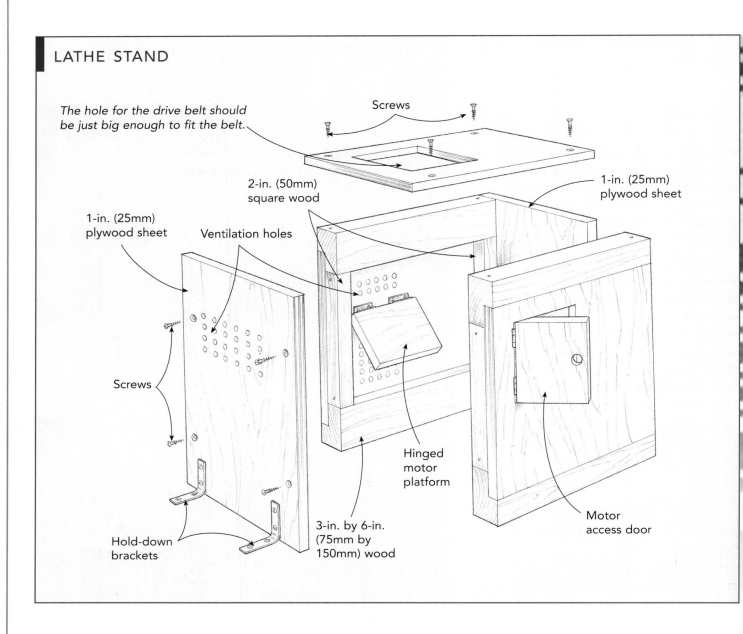

The hole for the drive belt should be just big enough to fit the belt.

Screws

2-in. (50mm) square wood

1-in. (25mm) plywood sheet

1-in. (25mm) plywood sheet

Ventilation holes

Screws

Hold-down brackets

3-in. by 6-in. (75mm by 150mm) wood

Hinged motor platform

Motor access door

• **The tailstock** Although not used much in connection with box turning, you'll need a tailstock sooner or later for something. The body should be cast iron and easy to move along the lathe bed. You must be able to lock it firmly in position using a single lever, which remains in place like the cam-action lever (see the photos on p. 5). Separate wrenches are annoying to use and get lost in shavings. The handwheel, which adjusts quill travel, should be easy to rotate; a

little handle makes it easy to wind. The quill should travel at least 2½ in. (65mm) on the mini lathes and 4 in. (100mm) on larger machines.

• **The centers** The lathe centers must be in exactly the same plane, which is not always the case even on new machines. You can check this by running the lathe with a short length of wood mounted in a scroll chuck. Lock the tail-

Switches need to be readily accessible
in case anything goes wrong.

stock in place so the center is ³⁄₁₆ in. (5mm) away from the wood, then turn the handwheel until the tailstock center just touches the wood. If the center point is off center, it will leave a circle on the wood in the chuck. If it's true, it will leave a cone.

• **The tool-rest assembly** This very important part of the lathe needs to provide solid support for the tool because any vibration or flexing in the rest assembly is magnified at the cutting edge. Look for cam-action levers or fixed wrenches and a firm clamping action. The tool rest is adjusted frequently, and searching for wrenches or Allen keys in shavings gets tedious. Life is too short for that.

• **The switches and motors** Switches need to be readily accessible in case anything goes wrong. There should be a big red button you can hit in an emergency and can reach easily with part of your body other than your hand. Simple on/off switches are not good if both your hands are occupied and you have to turn the lathe off in a hurry. My Vicmarc 300 has a reversing switch to the left of the red stop button and farther left is the variable-speed adjustment lever (see the top photo on p. 5). I have always powered my lathes with 1-hp motors without problems, although this is overkill for the mini lathe. Typically these are driven using ⅓-hp to ½-hp motors.

Lathe setup The center height should be about 2 in. (50mm) above your elbow as you stand normally. A grinder a step away is essential, and the tools to be used should be close by. Even though my tools get covered in shavings, I still prefer to keep them just over the lathe bed, where I can pick them up easily without breaking the work flow. Having each handle different makes them easy to identify.

Chucks

In the good old days everybody who made boxes used a self-centering three-jaw engineer's chuck like that shown on the left in the photo below. It was frequently a messy and painful affair, but eventually you learned to keep your fingers away from the chuck jaws and only caught your knuckles occasionally. The good old days got better in the late '70s, when the first commercial spigot chucks appeared similar to those shown at center and right in the photo below. These are often sold secondhand and

The first chucks used to turn boxes were the knuckle-smashing three-jaw engineer's chuck (left), followed by the less injurious spigot chucks (center and right).

No boxmaker should be without a scroll chuck. Two-inch jaws (left) come standard with most chucks, while larger (center) and grooved versions (right) are available as accessories.

work well, but commercially they were superseded in the late '80s by the woodturner's scroll chucks.

Scroll chucks remain the ultimate general-purpose woodturning chuck and are now regarded as being almost as essential to the craft as chisels and gouges. The grip is quick acting, accurate, and flexible over a range of diameters, and most manufacturers offer a wide range of accessories. Names to look for are Vicmarc, Nova, Axminster, and Oneway.

For box turning you need to be concerned only with the scroll chuck's ability to clamp around short lengths of wood. The standard 2-in. (50mm) jaws provided by most manufacturers are the most useful, but larger jaws are available for greater diameters, and there are grooved versions for a more powerful grip (see the top photo at left). The chuck's ability to grip square-section stock means you don't have to use a tail center, although it's safe practice to use tail support for as long as possible, especially for larger pieces of wood.

A scroll chuck can grip almost any shape. To hold the work as securely as possible, make sure the end grain sits flat against the base of the chuck.

Scroll chucks are adjusted on the lathe, but to operate them efficiently you must be able to lock the drive shaft, which lets you have one hand on the wood or blank and the other on the lever. If you are unable to lock your lathe drive shaft, consider buying a key-operated unit (see the unit on the right in the top left photo) designed specifically for that situation.

Although the scroll chuck can grip just about any odd shape, the stock is held more securely if the end grain sits flat against the jaw base (see the center photo at left). However, you don't always need to use the full length of the jaws, especially when mounting cylindrical stock. On most cylinders or partially turned blanks, I make a shoulder to abut the jaws (see the bottom photo at left). The shoulder/jaw contact almost eliminates the possibility of the work moving off-center unless you have a big catch, but more important, it allows the box to

Turning a shoulder on the end of a blank provides a solid purchase for the jaws. It also allows the blank to stand proud of the chuck, so it's easy to make the best use of all the wood.

tand proud of the chuck. So as work proceeds, ou can feel more of the wall thickness than ou could if the blank occupied the full depth f the chuck jaws. Throughout this book you'll ee a range of different jaw sets in action.

Saws

ou might survive without these near-essential oodworking tools, but I doubt it. If you can ocate small-diameter logs or offcuts, you'll get y using a small handsaw or bowsaw found in most home or craft workshops.

In my workshop I have both a table saw and a andsaw. The former is ideal for cutting squares nd docking the ends square to fit into a chuck, ut I tend to stick to the bandsaw because of its greater depth of cut. If you want only one saw, 'd recommend a small lightweight bandsaw with a depth of cut around 12 in. (300mm) (see the top photo at right). For many smaller bandsaws a riser-block kit is available to increase the depth of cut, which then enables you to break down small logs or thick boards easily.

Turning Tools

Here I'll explore the many uses for essential box-making tools. Specialist tools are dealt with in the relevant sections. This is not an in-depth how-to section, since I wrote in detail about technique in *Turning Wood with Richard Raffan* (The Taunton Press, 2001). If some of the techniques are new to you, don't risk them on a valuable blank. Get some scrap wood and practice your cuts; you can even design forms in the process described on pp. 38–39.

Since the early '80s, most turning tools have been made of high-speed steel (HSS), which will probably be marked on the blade. Most of the best tools still come from Sheffield, England, where there is a long tradition of manufacturing edge tools. Henry Taylor, Ashley Iles,

An ideal woodturner's bandsaw has a 10-in. to 12-in. (250mm to 300mm) depth of cut, with a 1-hp motor (or bigger if your power circuits and budget allow).

Basic turning tools of the boxmaker, from left to right: two different-size gouges, a skew chisel, a parting tool, and square-end and round-nose scrapers.

SHEAR CUTS

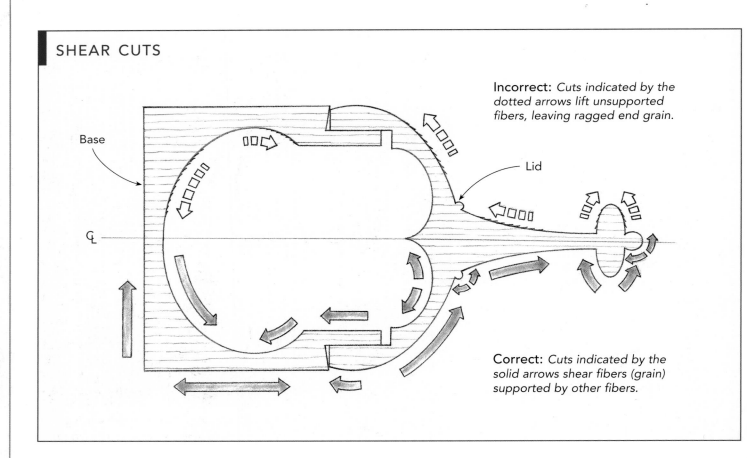

Incorrect: *Cuts indicated by the dotted arrows lift unsupported fibers, leaving ragged end grain.*

Base

Lid

C̵L

Correct: *Cuts indicated by the solid arrows shear fibers (grain) supported by other fibers.*

and Sorby are names long associated with the finest turning tools, and although other brands are beginning to nibble at their hold on the market, they rarely equal the overall quality. On my tools, I grind a basic 45° bevel and hone the top or flute to create a finer edge.

As you turn, try to remember the following:
- The best cut slices the wood fibers. Keep the portion of the edge doing the cutting at around 45° to the oncoming wood.
- Don't push the tool hard against the wood, especially when also against the axis.
- Keep a hand on the tool and tool rest: It's your point of reference for the cut as it proceeds.
- Fibers (grain) being cut should be supported by other fibers (see the drawing above).

GOUGES

The gouges used for all center work, including boxes, are shallow rather than deep fluted (see the photo at left on p. 12). They are used for roughing square-section stock to round blanks, for detailing, and for hollowing into the end grain. Grind your gouges to a fingernail-shaped end like the larger tool shown in the photo at right on p. 12. The pointed end of the smaller gouge severely limits the use of the tool, even though it is very good for fine detailing. The full convex curve of the larger tool is essential for hollowing end grain.

For roughing a square section to round, a 1-in. (25mm) gouge is ideal. A ½-in. (12mm) gouge does the job just as well but more slowly (see photo 1 on p. 11).

GOUGES

Center-work gouges show their versatility in box turning. Here are some key gouge techniques for turning square to round and cutting end grain.

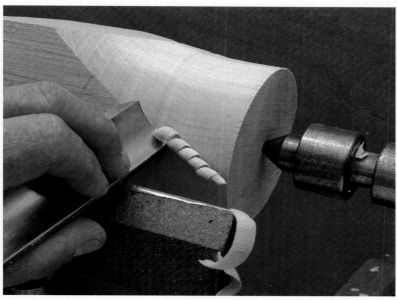

1 A 1-in. (25mm) roughing gouge makes quick work of bringing square sections to round.

3 I like to remove end grain quickly using the back-hollowing technique. The gouge works on its side and takes a shear cut away from the center to the right.

2 When turning end grain, you can take a heavier cut with a gouge than you can with a skew chisel.

4 A slower alternative to back hollowing is to take cuts in from the rim towards the center. The grain is likely to tear at the bottom of the curve.

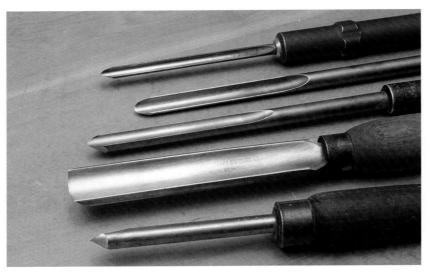

For better control while turning boxes, use shallow or half-round gouges for roughing, detailing, and hollowing. Grind the bevel to 45° or longer.

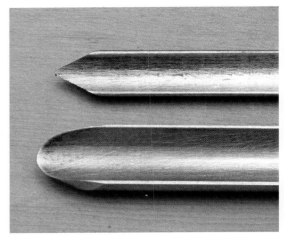

I've found the fingernail profile (bottom) is the best all-purpose grind. The pointier profile (top) is useful for detail work, but not for hollowing end grain or for roughing down.

HOLLOWING END GRAIN

Both back-hollowing and cutting into the end grain require scraping techniques to refine the curve.

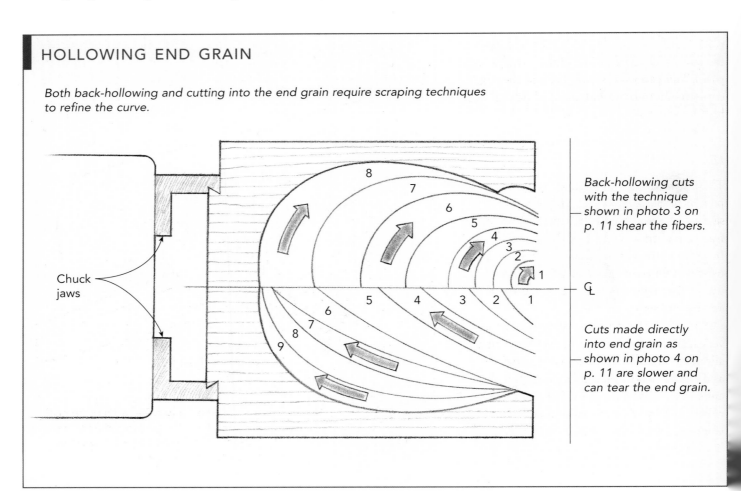

Chuck jaws

Back-hollowing cuts with the technique shown in photo 3 on p. 11 shear the fibers.

Cuts made directly into end grain as shown in photo 4 on p. 11 are slower and can tear the end grain.

On end grain you can take a heavier cut with a gouge than you can with a skew chisel. Keep the gouge almost on its side. If any part of the edge other than the nose of the tool touches the end grain, you'll have a dramatic catch (see photo 2 on p. 11).

There are two ways of hollowing end grain using a gouge. I go for the lightning-fast back-hollowing technique where the gouge works on its side, taking a shear cut away from the center to the right (see photo 3 on p. 11 and the upper section of the drawing on the facing page). The tool appears to be cutting upside down. This leaves an undulating surface to be cleaned up and refined using scrapers, but the waste is removed in seconds—once you've mastered the technique. You can practice while rough-turning (see p. 31).

Alternatively, you can take cuts in from the rim toward the center (see photo 4 on p. 11 and the lower section of the drawing on the facing page). This process is slower because the edge cuts straight into the end grain, while the back-hollowing cut slices the wood fibers.

Skew Chisels

These are the supreme tools for working grain parallel to the lathe axis. I grind mine with a slight curve, which broadens their use over the traditional straight edge (see the photo at right). In addition to the traditional shearing cuts, I use them for peeling and then in all sorts of ways where lightness of touch is essential if you are to avoid severe catches.

Shear cuts slice the fibers cleanly, leaving a very smooth surface. Keep the bevel rubbing at all times, and don't force the edge into or against the wood. If you get a ridged but cleanly cut surface off the tool, you don't have the bevel rubbing. Spiral chatter marks indicate that you're pushing too hard against the axis.

Skew chisels are the best tools for working grain parallel to the lathe axis. To broaden their usefulness, I prefer a slightly curved edge.

CUTTING END GRAIN

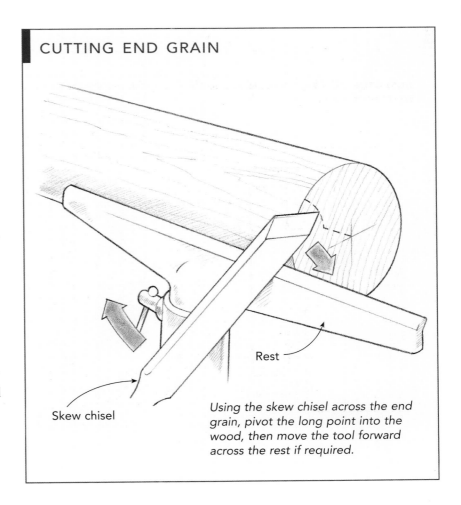

Rest

Skew chisel

Using the skew chisel across the end grain, pivot the long point into the wood, then move the tool forward across the rest if required.

SKEW CHISELS

1 & 2 A skew chisel can be used with the point up or down. The important thing is to keep the cutting edge at around 45° to the oncoming wood. A skew chisel used with a shear cut will leave an absolutely smooth surface. Be sure to take light cuts and don't force the tool into the wood.

3 & 4 To cut a dome with a skew chisel, start with the long point up then switch to the long point down as you work along the axis.

5 Use the skew chisel long point down for shearing across the grain. The tool is pointing in the direction you want to go and thus is easier to steer and less likely to catch.

6 When using the skew chisel for fine detailing, only the point and bevel side should contact the wood, not the edge.

7 Peeling cuts cannot be beaten for rapid waste removal. To peel, keep the tool flat on the rest and the edge just below the wood surface.

8 A peel/scrape cut will allow you to deal with twisted grain without causing tearout.

9 When shear-scraping in a corner, ease the short corner of the skew chisel gently into the work, rolling the tool counterclockwise to take a light cut.

10 You can scrape end grain with a skew chisel as long as you take a very delicate cut and keep the tool flat on the rest.

11 Use the bevel side to scrape an end-grain shoulder. Squeeze the tool into the wood to remove only powder. Hone the side of the tool as well as the bevel.

Rounded Boxes

Rounded forms are easier to open if slightly flattened on either side of the join. The hint of an ogee at the base of the smaller box makes it the more elegant of the two.

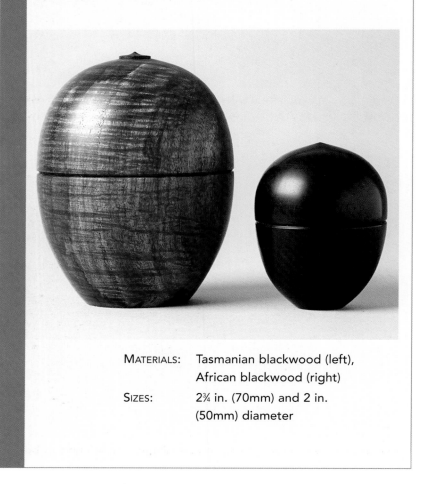

MATERIALS: Tasmanian blackwood (left), African blackwood (right)

SIZES: 2¾ in. (70mm) and 2 in. (50mm) diameter

Never use the long point of a skew chisel down at the start of a curve or for cutting beads.

Remember, you can use a skew chisel with the long point up or down, but the portion of the edge slicing the wood needs to lie at about 45° to the oncoming wood to work effectively. If a sharp edge doesn't cut freely, check for this angle first.

When cutting curves, start with the long point of the skew chisel up, but flip the tool over and continue with the long point down so you can see what is happening as you work more against the axis. Never use the long point down at the start of a curve or for cutting beads.

Use the skew chisel long point down across the grain (see the drawing on p. 13). This allows you to see what you're doing, and catches are less traumatic.

For fine detailing, pin the tool to the rest using a secure grip, then raise the handle to pivot the point into the wood. Only the point and bevel side contact the wood. If the edge touches the end grain, you risk a dramatic catch.

Peel/scrape cuts are pretty sneaky, being not quite a scrape, not quite a peel. But it's my favorite way of dealing with really twisted grain without the risk of it picking out. Go very gently so you barely brush the surface of the wood. Any force will induce a bad catch and pull the work off-center if not out of the chuck. When cutting a shoulder, a slight curve to the edge of the skew chisel allows you to use just the point without the rest of the edge catching.

Shear scraping ensures crispness to fine detailing on very hard end grain. In such situations I start with the skew chisel flat on its side. The idea is to ease the corner of the tool into the end grain to take the merest wisp of a shaving, then to roll it counterclockwise to present the edge at an angle to the end grain. This cut is used in extremely delicate situations, such as when completing a lid or base that is held by friction (rather than by a chuck). You might need to support the job with your left hand while easing the tool very gently into the wood with the right. If you push too hard, the edge will catch the wood and pull it loose, but with your hand there, you can catch it and ease it back on.

I use the skew chisel flat on the rest to scrape end grain, so I cannot exert too much pressure against the wood. Think in terms of stroking the surface with the edge: Don't use force. If you don't get dustlike shavings, go to the grinder and touch the underside bevel to raise a small burr (which will face upward when cutting).

PARTING TOOLS AND DEPTH DRILL

I prefer a diamond-shaped parting tool, which I find the least likely to bind (see the top photo at right). Depth drills are easily made by inserting a drill into a handle. I grind on marks to help gauge the depth as I drill.

SCRAPERS

In the context of end-grain boxes and the center-work techniques covered in this book, scrapers are strictly for internal use. In general, don't bother with them for any external shaping: You'll tear the grain or have a bad catch. When you need to scrape on the outside of a box, you'll have more control using a skew chisel. However, for internal shaping, scrapers are the only tools that enable you to get cleanly cut surfaces exactly where you want them, especially on very hard woods. There are still people who think that the use of scrapers signifies a lack of skill, a notion that seems to have sprung up in the '60s. Pity these ignoramuses: They either lack the skills to get the best from scraping techniques or are too blinkered to try.

Scrapers can be difficult to use, particularly as you deep-hollow when there is a lot of lever-

Parting tools can be useful for detailing as well as for parting off (center and bottom). Depth drills enable you to establish depths for hollowing quickly (top).

Scrapers are essential for shaping and cleaning up the interiors of boxes.

age to control. The secret, as with all turning, is not to force the tool against the wood. For finishing cuts, aim to stroke the surface lightly with pressure akin to lightly rubbing your hands together. Keep the tool flat on the rest at all times, using no more than half the edge at once or less if turning very hard woods.

SCRAPING END GRAIN

Scrapers should be used so that if they catch, the edge will travel into space.

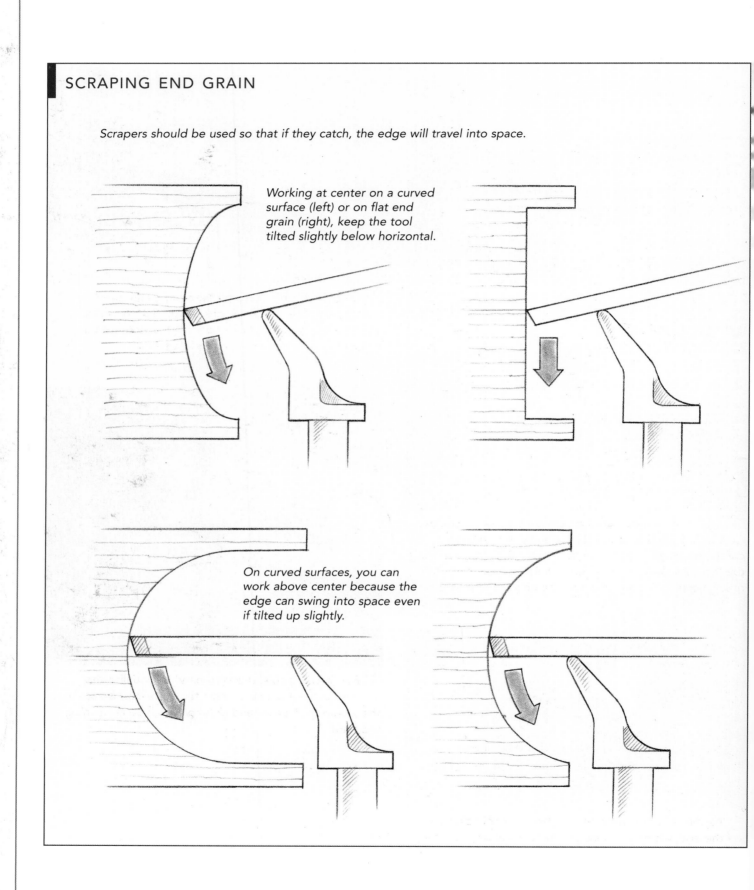

Working at center on a curved surface (left) or on flat end grain (right), keep the tool tilted slightly below horizontal.

On curved surfaces, you can work above center because the edge can swing into space even if tilted up slightly.

SCRAPERS

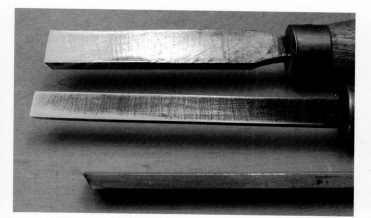

4 Keep the bevels steep on the sides of radiused scrapers. The center bevel will work into confined spaces but is ground too far back on the side, making it likely to catch when used on side grain.

1 & 2 My square-end scrapers are very rarely square. I grind a very slight arc away from the left corner, which gives me an extra-sharp corner while making the tool less likely to grab during finishing cuts on end grain. Never use more than half the edge at one time.

5 For finishing cuts, use your hand to equalize the pressure of the tool against the wood and dampen the vibration. If your hand gets too hot, you're pushing too hard.

3 Asymmetrical scrapers should have a long bevel on the end, which steepens to near vertical on the side.

One of the attractions of turning boxes

is that you don't need too much equipment.

My square-end scrapers very rarely are square. I grind a very slight arc away from the left corner, which gives me an extra-sharp corner while making the tool less likely to grab during finishing cuts on end grain. Use square-end scrapers horizontally or tilted slightly down (see the drawing on p. 18), never upward.

Just like my non-square-end scrapers, my roundnose scrapers are rarely round. I grind them to more of an asymmetrical shape for greater control when cutting side grain. With thicker scrapers you'll need a secondary or long bevel on the end of the tool so that it can work in confined spaces. The side of the bevel should be kept steep; otherwise the tool becomes too aggressive and catches easily.

On side-grain cuts near the rim, you get a better finish using a roundnose scraper tilted up. Have the rest at center height. Pay particular attention to the way the left hand sits on the rest with the fingers dampening the vibrating wood. Note that the tool blade is pushed against the thumb, which resists (see photo 5 on p. 19). The idea is to set up opposing forces, with your left thumb pushing to the right to modify the motion of the tool, which is being pushed forward and slightly left by the right hand. As you move the tool forward across the rest, raise the handle to bring the edge through an arc into the cut. Working from center you can lower the handle slightly to get the hint of a shear cut as the edge swings left.

Ancillary Tools

One of the attractions of turning boxes is that you don't need too much equipment. So in the small-tool department you'll need only a couple of sets of calipers, a ruler, a grinder, cyanoacrylate glue, and abrasives. Don't waste money on expensive vernier calipers, but avoid the plastic ones; they melt when held against revolving wood. There are always cheap metal versions around that are ideal and can stand the abuse of constant use.

GRINDER

My first grinder, bought on a tight budget, had 6-in. (150mm) carborundum wheels, and I used it for at least 10 years. It enabled me to keep my edges sharp, although they looked appalling, with multifaceted bevels on the thicker tools. A larger wheel is easier to use and produces a better-looking bevel, so these days I use 8-in. (200mm) 36-grit and 80-grit white wheels suited to high-speed steel. The rough-looking bit of wood on the right-side rest in the photo on the facing page is stuck on to cover the drill-grinding V groove beneath. It works well as a rest.

The most desirable feature for a grinder is that it picks up speed quickly when switched on; otherwise you have to stand around waiting for it. Some grinders take several seconds to pick up speed, adding up to wasted minutes of waiting around each day and wasted hours to days over the years.

A wheel dresser is essential for keeping the wheel true and sharp. The only ones worth considering are the diamond wheel dressers. They are uninspiring tools to look at, being small blocks of diamond amalgam, but they are one of the best tools you can have in a workshop with a grinder.

CYANOACRYLATE GLUE

I lost count long ago of the many boxes that split and then aborted. In the past, I threw the bits away and started afresh. These days there's cyanoacrylate glue, commonly known as Super Glue. If you have any split that vanishes when squeezed tight, it can be fixed and nobody needs to know. The repair technique for splits is to align both sides of the split and run a thin band of cyanoacrylate into the crack, then quickly squeeze it tight and spray it with accelerator. It will set in about five seconds.

To fill gaps or defects, squirt some accelerator into the hole to be filled, pack the hole tight with dust, and flow thin cyanoacrylate glue over the top. The adhesive percolates instantly through the dust, hits the accelerator, and starts setting. I give another squirt of accelerator to the outside, and there you have it—it looks just like solid wood. No woodworker should be without this glue.

ABRASIVES

Go for soft, flexible, lightweight cloth-backed abrasives ranging from a coarse 80 grit to a fine 400 grit or 600 grit. I use 100, 150, 220, 320, and 400 grits. Cloth-backed abrasives are more expensive than the paper-backed type, but they cut better, last longer, tear easily into strips, and don't crack or form hard corners when folded. For still finer surfaces I use 0000 wire wool (also known as steel wool) or abrasive sanding pads.

A small bench grinder is a must for keeping your tools correctly shaped and sharpened. Wheel dressers (left) keep the grinding wheels running true and prevent them from clogging.

Dust Collection and Safety

Dust is a major health hazard, and the most injurious to your lungs is the stuff you cannot see. When I started turning in 1970 it was in a workshop filled with suspended dust, which eventually settled on every surface. Every morning it lay knee-high to a spider on the bandsaw table wiped clean the previous day, and on shelves and power cables it piled up a finger thick. Had it been snow it would have been picturesque.

I soon took to wearing a dust mask, unlike my companion who stood at his lathe smoking his pipe while generating more dust. Then in his late 30s, he had major lung problems, and the slightest cold sank to his chest and had him off work for weeks. For my workshop, I bought a dust-collection system the moment I could

You should always wear a face shield unless turning miniatures,
when safety glasses should be sufficient to protect your eyes.

Face shields should be worn whenever you work at a lathe, although safety spectacles to protect your eyes are probably sufficient when turning miniatures.

afford it; this machine is as essential as a band-saw and lathe. There are a number of good small systems, and you should buy as good a one as you can afford.

In addition, I have for many years lived my working day in the battery-powered Racal Airstream helmet (see the helmet at right in the photo above). It contains a mini fan and filters the air I breathe while protecting me from the occasional lump of flying wood. There are a

number of helmets commercially available. I prefer the fan in the helmet rather than in a waist pack. I consider a visor that I can tilt up essential so I can take a closer look at something without having to remove the whole helmet.

You should always wear a face shield unless turning miniatures, when safety glasses should be sufficient to protect your eyes. A couple of years back I failed to use a face shield when finishing a small box. The chuck—a 2-in. (50mm) square 6 in. (150mm) long—hit me and I had to have 13 stitches in my forehead. I was lucky; I could have lost an eye or some teeth.

To help ensure safety, light must be good. Ideally you'd have really good natural lighting, but few of us do, especially working at night. Get good general lighting and have an angle lamp that you can move around to bring light onto the work as required. When dealing with form, you need shadow as well as light, and it is helpful if this can be manipulated.

If you work with good tools in good condition and pay attention to safety procedures, you should manage to keep all your fingers in their rightful places, suffering only the odd nick on your hands from flying chips. But try to develop the habit of stopping for a moment before you do anything to ask yourself what the consequences of your actions are likely to be. If you are not sure, proceed with even more caution than you should be using anyway.

2 WOOD SELECTION & PREPARATION

The creation of a finely turned box demands stable material. Any warping in a completed box will affect both the visual and tactile qualities of how the lid fits over the base. It might jam or loosen, but either way the box will look terrible along the line where the lid and base meet. Consequently, it pays to learn how to choose wood best suited to box making and then to learn how to cut and dry it so that you end up with an almost inert box blank. As you will see later in this chapter, the last step in drying is to partially turn your blanks so that you'll have fewer problems both in the making and then further down the line with the finished object.

Because small boxes are made from short, square-section lengths, you can regard almost any small chunk of wood as a potential blank provided it's free of splits and rot and has moderately tight grain. Even though you can use just about any wood, in general it's best to choose species known for their stability.

Types of Wood

Trees are classified as deciduous or coniferous but known commonly as hardwoods or softwoods, respectively. In general, hardwoods are slower growing, denser, and heavier than the lighter-weight and more open-grained softwoods. As a professional turner, I look for woods that won't present too many problems. Life is too short to be fighting with any wood widely acknowledged as difficult to cut or finish cleanly. Very hard wood can be stressful to work, especially on the end grain, where catches can be ferocious. But these catches can be controlled and the surface cut cleanly, whereas the end grain encountered in many softwoods will always tear out.

Most of my favorite woods are the dense-grained hardwoods of the Acacia and Dalbergia (rosewood) families and fruit woods, all long favored for intricate turnery. Some softwoods, such as yew, huon pine, or even radiata pine,

Life is too short to be fighting with any wood widely acknowledged as difficult to cut or finish cleanly.

Avoid open-structured lumber with broadly spaced growth rings (left). This type of wood is guaranteed to tear out. The other blanks, however, are practically ideal, with hardly any splits.

can be equally satisfying to work. I avoid lumber that has well-spaced and well-defined growth rings with fluffy open-structured wood between, such as spruce, fir, and many of the pines. (For a typical example of what to avoid, see the left board standing on edge in the photo above.) Such grain is guaranteed to tear out, no matter how you cut it, how delicate your touch, or how efficient your abrasive. Working with this kind of grain is akin to using balsa or some near-rotten spalted wood, which never allows you to create more than a second-rate object unless the wood is soaked in resin, which in turn raises the specter of dust and lung problems.

The other blanks shown in the photo above are nearly ideal. On the bottom right is a block of huon pine, a dense straight-grained softwood from Tasmania with a patch of a bird's-eye figure within the pencil outline. This could be tricky to work but should polish up beautifully. The pair of blanks at the top are laburnum, each with a strong end-grain pattern, which will

look wonderful on the top of a box. (You can see how a similar blank finished up on p. 57.)

For more detailed information about woods, you'll find much published not only in books but also in many woodworking magazines. Over the years, I've collected a fair number of reference books in secondhand bookstores, often picking up a batch from an estate. Another wonderful source of help, information, and inspiration is your local woodworking or wood-turning club. With the revived interest in handicrafts, thousands of such organizations have been set up for the sharing of information, and there are always members eager to help those less experienced than themselves. And now there's the Internet, too.

Sourcing Wood

I have very rarely had to buy wood specifically for boxes. Typically I use scraps of wood that many woodworkers would expect to discard, which is great news if you're on a tight budget and is very sound ecologically. It is rare to find a seasoned board that hasn't split while drying, and I, like most woodworkers, tend to lop off the end to get back to solid wood. In my case, this is usually thick stock for bowls. But rather than throw away the offcut, I save it and work between the splits, cutting out short, squared lengths (see the photo on the facing page). Short ends that might otherwise be wasted yield a heap of box material. If you're new to woodworking and don't have your own pile of offcuts yet, seek out a lumberyard or go hunting with a bowsaw for tree loppings and such.

Everywhere I've been I've noticed trees being chopped down and logs and branches being carted away for disposal. Often people will be delighted to have you make use of what is otherwise rubbish or firewood. There is a good deal of wonderful material in the trunks of woody shrubs like laurel, cotoneaster, or rhododendron, which have trunks of dense close-grained wood that rarely splits during seasoning and can have fine patterns on the end grain. Many of these shrubs will retain the bark. Such woods are rarely found in lumberyards, so you need to keep your eyes open for people clearing out gardens or pruning shrubs. Look for solid wood with virtually no sap or splits. And if a friend gives you a log or two, don't forget to give your friend one of your turnings in return—then you might be remembered the next time he or she goes pruning.

Since the mid '80s, we woodturners have been well served by a number of mail-order stores dedicated to our particular needs. They advertise in the woodworking press, and in addition to all the tools and accessories, many offer a range of top-quality hardwoods in small sections cut for specific projects, or even packs of mixed woods so that you can try a range of species. This is about as good a source as you will find for small quantities of special or unusual woods.

For larger quantities of squared lumber or logs, you might try one of the specialist dealers who cater to cabinetmakers and woodworkers. You'll find their advertisements in woodworking magazines and the Yellow Pages. They will all ship orders, but you might be lucky enough to have a dealer on your doorstep. It's always preferable to be able to see what you're buying when things get really expensive, as they will if you start buying logs of tropical hardwood, which are very heavy and typically sold by weight. Logs should always be less expensive than sawn lumber, but with the latter you know exactly what you are getting.

Logs are often a gamble, but they can reveal spectacular grain patterns and color when opened up. You can get a hint of what's inside by looking carefully at the end-grain patterns and for defects on the sides that might indicate bark intrusions or rot. Watch out for worm holes. Smooth, round logs will generally provide clean, straight-grained wood. The more interest-

Logs are often a gamble, but they can reveal spectacular grain patterns and color when opened up.

One of the best sources for blanks for box making is your offcut bin. Cut your odd lumps into square-section lengths and set them aside to dry.

ing grain patterns come from around bends and undulating surfaces, where the wood is under tension. But be warned: It is around really twisted and interesting grain that the wood is most likely to split. The best usually lurks on the edge of disaster.

Cutting Wood for Blanks

How the grain—by which I mean the fibers of the wood as they lie in the tree parallel to the pith and bark—lies in the blank will greatly affect the long-term stability of the finished box. As wood dries, the length hardly alters, but shrinkage across the grain can be 5% to 6% or more. Changing humidity, which comes with the seasons, central heating, or sudden thunderstorms, will cause any wood, including boxes, to shrink and swell. But if you have the grain run-

To ensure the top and base of your box fit together and remain flat over time, the grain should run the length of a box blank.

ning from the top to the bottom of your box, the crucial rims where the top and base fit together tend to remain flat, even though the diameter will shrink to be somewhat oval. Boxes with cross-grain will not only shrink to an oval but also cup, making a lid that fits tightly an unlikely prospect. Consequently, the grain should run the length of a box blank (see the photo at left).

If you need further persuasion to avoid cross-grain, you'll find that the end grain on small-diameter projects, almost regardless of wood species, is nearly impossible to cut cleanly unless the wood is particularly close grained.

In addition to grain direction, you should also be aware of the mix of heartwood to sapwood in your lumber. Traditionally, sapwood was milled out because it is what bugs and critters head for. On most lumber I think this

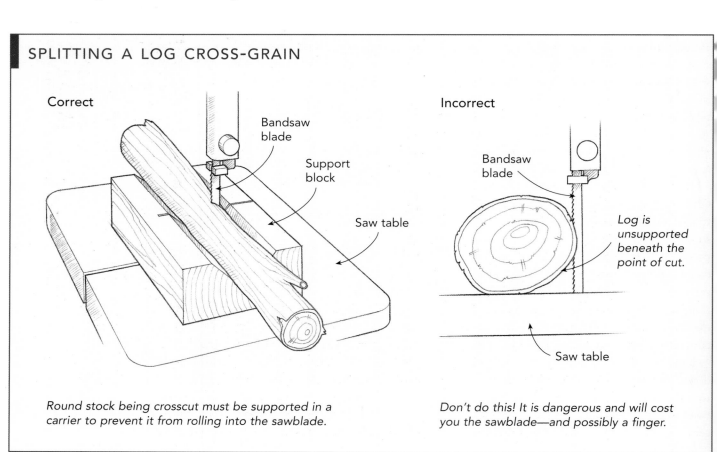

SPLITTING A LOG CROSS-GRAIN

Correct

Bandsaw blade

Support block

Saw table

Round stock being crosscut must be supported in a carrier to prevent it from rolling into the sawblade.

Incorrect

Bandsaw blade

Log is unsupported beneath the point of cut.

Saw table

Don't do this! It is dangerous and will cost you the sawblade—and possibly a finger.

remains the best policy because the last thing you want is wood borers in your lumber pile, let alone the partly finished or finished product. However, some species have the most gorgeous contrast between sapwood and heartwood. African blackwood leaps to mind, along with cocobolo, gidgee, and yew, but there are many others. If you can get to the wood before the bugs, you can probably keep them out. I use insect bombs regularly in my wood storage area and have had few problems.

Small logs or branches are most safely broken down into smaller pieces using a bowsaw, although a chainsaw is quicker. I have a small electric model that I use in the workshop. Regardless of what you use to cut the log or branch, never attempt to cut round stock without a sawhorse, carrier, block, or wedges to stop the stock from rolling.

When converting either boards or logs to squared lumber, make sure that you eliminate all splits and evidence of woodworm (generally confined to the sap). Splits can be difficult to spot, especially when cutting away the defective end of a log or board. After cutting away a split, take a very thin test slice of just ⅛ in. (2mm) and bend it. It will break on any split (see the photo on p. 28), so take another test slice and another until you have one free of defects.

I always assume that I'll lose up to 1 in. (25mm) of the end grain from green wood due to splitting during the first few months of seasoning, so I cut freshly sawn squares as long as possible. After six to eight months the moisture content should drop to 18% to 20%, and you can cut to shorter lengths if need be with little chance of more end-grain checking. I have an electronic moisture meter to check moisture content, which is handy, but not essential.

As early as possible in the process of breaking down a log, you should create a face so the wood can sit flat on a saw table. There are only two ways to do this safely without risking a finger or two. For long lengths being split in two

Blackwood Group

When the sapwood contrasts so dramatically with the heartwood, it needs to flow through the join as if unbroken. African blackwood is one of the finest box-turning woods. It polishes brilliantly.

MATERIAL: African blackwood
SIZE: 1¾ in. (45mm) diameter

on the bandsaw, use wedges, or angled blocks, to support the log (see the drawing on p. 28). For safety, the cut must be near the center of the log. Never attempt to take a thin lengthwise slice from a log unless you have properly engineered dogs and carriage to grip the log.

The second, safest way to create a flat surface on a round log is to push a short length set on end through the bandsaw, usually along the line of the major split. The disadvantage is that you get only short lengths, but it is a very safe way of cutting because the log sits square on the saw table. I will often cut the whole piece this way because I find it very easy to gauge the squares by eye, but there is a fire hazard in the sawdust. As the saw teeth travel along the grain they create a wood wool, which can be ignited by sparks that can occur if the blade is forced against the guides. Stop the bandsaw every few minutes to check the buildup of dust within the saw. If you smell burning, stop the saw immediately.

It pays to cut a very thin test slice from the end of a blank and bend it. If it breaks, take additional slices until you get one that's free of defects.

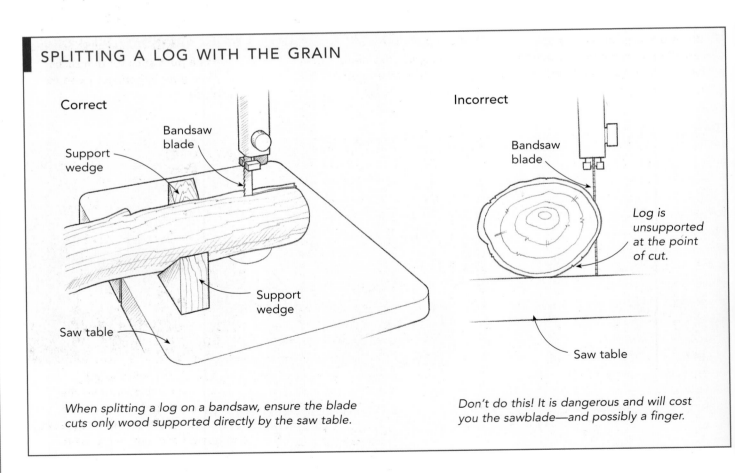

SPLITTING A LOG WITH THE GRAIN

Correct

Support wedge

Bandsaw blade

Support wedge

Saw table

When splitting a log on a bandsaw, ensure the blade cuts only wood supported directly by the saw table.

Incorrect

Bandsaw blade

Log is unsupported at the point of cut.

Saw table

Don't do this! It is dangerous and will cost you the sawblade—and possibly a finger.

CONVERTING A SMALL LOG TO SQUARES

1 This offcut of a laburnum log is 10 years old and bone dry. Most logs have some splits radiating from the pith even when newly felled. You should make an initial cut along the main split.

2 If the split goes deeper than expected, take another slice to remove the defect.

3 Use a push stick for thin slices when your fingers get close to the blade.

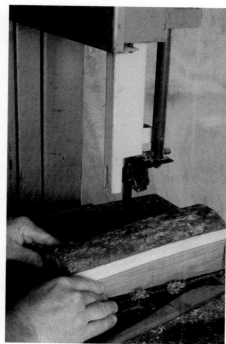

4, 5 & 6 With the split removed, lay the half log on its side and cut out a squared length. Note that the guides and guard have been lowered for safety and that I keep my fingers clear of the blade.

Nesting Boxes

When making a set of nesting boxes, you'll frequently have odd boxes left over like the two left front. Make the innermost box first, then the next just large enough to hold it.

MATERIAL:	Cocobolo
SIZES:	2 in. (50mm) maximum diameter

Sometimes, to speed up drying slightly, I reduce the squares to cylinders. The only disadvantage to this is that it limits the uses of the blanks.

Air-Drying Blanks

You can soon build up a good stockpile by scavenging and saving offcuts, but the blanks will need to be dried to ensure their stability. This means keeping them out of the direct sun but well aired. The rule of thumb for drying lumber is one year for every 1 in. (25mm) of thickness plus a year. Thus for 1-in. (25mm) squares you should allow two years for drying, for 2-in. (50mm) squares three years, and so on. To speed up drying somewhat, I occasionally reduce the squares to cylinders (see the photo above right), but this starts to limit their uses. Commercially, I might regret committing all my stock to boxes when little bowls might be selling better in a few years' time, so these days I keep the lumber square and solid. I store longer lengths in a loose bundle in my basement, but any shady, cool, and breezy spot will do. Very short pieces I keep tossed (not packed or stacked) in open-weave sacks and cardboard boxes.

Air-drying takes time, and for that reason most lumber used for commercial woodworking is kiln dried, which speeds up the process but alters the structure of the lumber, making it quite unpleasant to work. In addition, the chemicals often used with many kiln-drying processes make for particularly unhealthy dust, especially when sanding. I have always preferred air-dried material, which seems to get better with age. I have been lucky enough to work oak and elm known to be hundreds of years old; it was a magical experience that taught me you can't keep wood drying long enough.

Remember, you can reasonably expect to lose at least 1 in. (25mm) from each end of lumber sawn from green logs due to splitting, even in very stable woods. To limit such degradation, it is common practice to coat the ends with a wood sealer, an inexpensive waxy emulsion readily available from woodturners' supply merchants. But I have found that this slows up rather than prevents the splitting process, so I often rough-turn blanks to speed the drying, which virtually eliminates splitting.

Rough-Turning

Rough-turning a blank enables you to speed up drying and allows you to finish a piece from green wood within a few months. I have many rough-turned blanks that are up to 10 years old sitting around in crates and bags ready to go but getting better still with age. The idea is that you turn each section of the box, leaving a wall thickness of around ½ in. (15mm) (see the drawing at right). Then you tape these top to bottom so that the air can circulate around each end (see the photo at right).

During the rough-hollowing be sure to keep track of the lid and base sections so that in the final box the grain pattern flows from top to bottom. This is easy working with a single blank, provided you turn a small shoulder on either end (see the drawing on p. 32). When the blank is parted in two, the shoulders locate the top of the lid and the bottom of the base section, making it easy to keep the pieces aligned as they were in the log. If your design demands that you work with a shoulderless blank, scribble a line or two across your intended parting cut so you can be sure to keep the wood aligned correctly. This practice is good insurance anyway against the time you or the cat knocks all your parted blanks on the floor just before you get to hollow them.

Rough-turned blanks will dry quicker than those that haven't been turned. To ensure that the grain pattern flows from top to bottom in the final box, keep track of the lid and base sections during rough-hollowing. Once the pieces are hollowed, tape the lid and base sections together so air can circulate around each end.

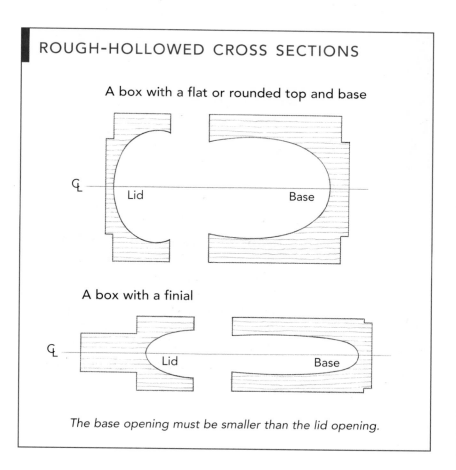

ROUGH-HOLLOWED CROSS SECTIONS

A box with a flat or rounded top and base

℄ Lid   Base

A box with a finial

℄ Lid   Base

The base opening must be smaller than the lid opening.

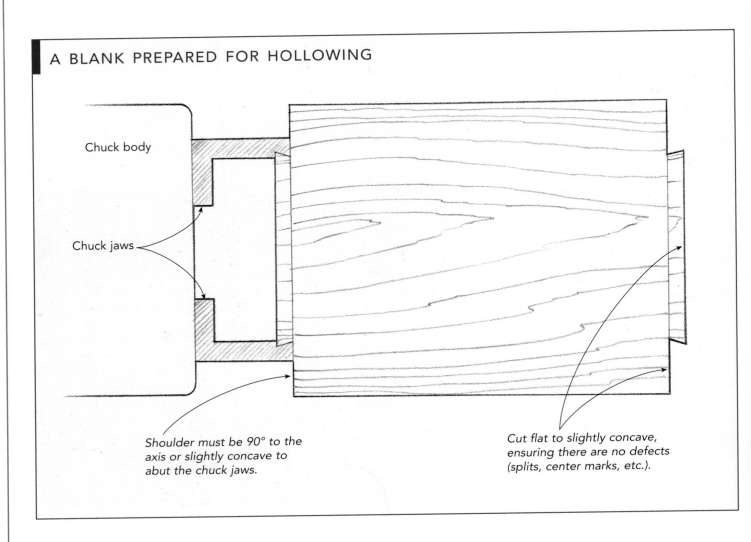

A BLANK PREPARED FOR HOLLOWING

Chuck body

Chuck jaws

Shoulder must be 90° to the axis or slightly concave to abut the chuck jaws.

Cut flat to slightly concave, ensuring there are no defects (splits, center marks, etc.).

Preparing Blanks

You could remove the center of the boxes with a drill, but this is an excellent opportunity for honing your gouge technique and is probably faster. Using the back-hollowing method (see photo 8 on p. 35), it takes only a few seconds to remove the bulk of the inside. As work proceeds, always get rid of everything you don't want in the finished piece, like splits or marks from the spur drive, as early as possible. It is very easy to forget to make allowances for damaged end grain as you hollow your lid or base, only to discover too late that you don't have enough wood left to finish the outside properly.

INDIVIDUAL BLANKS

How you attack your squared lumber, branches, or small logs depends on the chuck or chucks at your disposal. If your chuck has jaws that allow you to grip the blank, then use the chuck. The advantage is that you can true the ends and leave them free of blemishes, whereas turning a blank held between centers damages the end grain. I turn a small shoulder on each end of the blank, not only to keep track of the tops and bottoms but also because I rarely need to use the full depth of the jaws offered by most chucks. The chucks will hold firmly on as little as ⅛ in. (3mm), provided you leave a supportive shoulder for the jaw to abut.

Alternatively, after truing the end grain, you can save wood by separating the lid and base on the bandsaw, using the square section of the blank to prevent it from being pulled into the sawblade (see the photo at right). Then rechuck the square section by gripping it at the rounded end and turn a shoulder on the other end.

If your chuck jaws are unable to accommodate the squared blank, you'll have to mount the blank between centers initially in order to turn a shoulder you can grip. Here are the steps:

1. Mount the blank between centers and rough it to round, leaving a ⅜-in.- (10mm) long shoulder that fits your chuck at either end. The cones of the spur drive and tail center will penetrate the blank, so you'll lose about half of each shoulder at either end.

2. Mount the blank in the chuck and turn away the damaged ends, ensuring that the end grain is free of blemishes.

3. Cut the blank in half on the lathe using a parting tool.

4. Rough-hollow the lid section.

5. Rough-hollow the base section, being careful not to widen the opening too much (see the drawing on p. 31).

MULTIPLE BLANKS FROM ONE LENGTH

To save valuable wood and time, I often prepare a number of blanks from a single length of lumber, dividing individual base and lid sections on the bandsaw. There are three advantages: First, I have only two ends damaged by the lathe centers, whereas if I cut the length to individual blanks, I could have similar waste on each blank. Second, a number of parting cuts on a length would be difficult to handle and could cause the length to break, which could be dangerous. And finally, the bandsaw cut is much thinner than the parting tool's. Cutting a cylinder on the bandsaw is dangerous, so you must use a carrier or leave a square section on the cylinder to do it.

To save valuable wood and time, I often prepare a number of blanks from a single length of lumber.

An alternative way to part blanks that saves wood is to separate the lid and base on the bandsaw, using the square section of the blank to prevent it from being pulled and rolled into the sawblade.

Finally, when finishing boxes from solid (as opposed to rough-turned) blanks, I still rough-turn both the lid and base, no matter how old and well seasoned the lumber. Over the years I've learned that the hollowing alters the structure and stresses within any blank and that some minuscule movement is almost inevitable. By partly turning both sections and leaving them for a couple of hours before chucking up the lid section for the final turning, I make the material as stable as I can. Once you have the parts roughed out, you can move on to the more exacting task of final turning.

PREPARING AN INDIVIDUAL BLANK

1 This square blank is gripped by the jaws and ready for roughing.

2 Reduce the square to a cylinder.

3 True the end grain.

4 Turn a shoulder to fit your chuck.

5 Reverse the blank and repeat the process.

6 Check for defects. Mark the splits and turn them away.

7 Separate the lid and base sections using a parting tool.

8 Rough-hollow each section.

PREPARING MULTIPLE BLANKS

1 The piece here is turned and ready for dividing on the bandsaw. To the left, I'll cut on the lines, creating short cylinders I can hold in my step-jaw chuck. To the right, the blanks will be held in 2-in. (50mm) jaws.

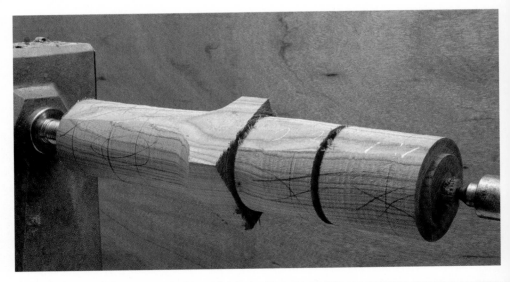

2 Here you can see how the square section prevents the otherwise cylindrical blank from rolling into the blade. On the lid section of the blank already cut, I forgot to trim the end, but that can easily be done on the lathe.

3 The lid and base in the front center are hollowed and taped for drying. The others are ready to be hollowed. At the rear center, what looks destined to be a lid could be used for a flat box.

CHAPTER

3 DESIGN

Turned boxes are seldom spectacular. Their small scale seems to deny them that opportunity granted to other products from the lathe. Rather, they are objects to be discovered with a growing appreciation as they are handled. Almost every turned box fits easily into an adult hand, so the tactile qualities—how it feels—are important. Is it well balanced or top-heavy? Is it leaden in the base or too lightweight?

Much of what we think will be based on an almost subliminal assessment of the form as we approach it. If it looks top-heavy, very likely we will be inclined to feel that. If the looks are not matched by the way the piece feels, we are left feeling dissatisfied, cheated even, unless there is some form of joke or visual pun on the part of the maker.

In the early '70s, during my formative years as a turner, I made boxes with straight sides, flat or domed lids with big knobs, and a nice suction fit to the lid. Like the other turners I knew, I made little or no attempt to match the grain

because we all knew it couldn't be done. The inside shape echoed the profile, and the walls were fairly thin. These boxes sold quite well but were prosaic with the grain differences between the lid and base detracting from the whole. Then suddenly we turners saw how to line up the grain top to bottom, and the boxes improved because the patterns no longer jarred the eye. Spurred on by this, we broke away from the straight sides and began experimenting.

Since then I've explored a number of differing forms, gradually moving from one idea to another. For a few years past, I have been trying to emulate some antique Japanese and Korean ceramic tea jars I discovered. And writing this book is a tremendous spur to venture into all manner of forms and concepts. In general, I make boxes with over-fitting lids (rather than in-fitting) because I find them more satisfactory aesthetically and they offer technical advantages as turning proceeds. (There is more about the relative merits of each scenario in chapter 5.)

Almost every turned box fits easily into an adult hand,

so the tactile qualities—how it feels—are important.

I make dozens of similar forms to explore a theme. In this series I explored lid variations. Macassar ebony; c. 1992; 2 in. (50mm) in diameter.

A quick way to try different shapes is to turn them as solid forms. Almost any wood will do for this—unattractive scraps, odd branches, whatever is lying around the workshop.

Exploring Form

To translate vague concepts into a three-dimensional object on the lathe, I do some drawing, but for standard turned boxes I mostly work out my forms as I go along. Working in a series, I make dozens of similar boxes to explore a theme (see the photo above). From the series, I select those that I see as the most successful, and they become the benchmark for future efforts.

When teaching, I've noticed that people get into tremendous difficulties either because their skill level cannot fulfill their aspirations or because they have no goal or design in mind. You need to set out with some idea of the form you want to make, be it spherical, tapered with legs, or a simple cylinder. You can deviate if circumstances insist, such as when a defect in the wood means you have to change your ideas or when you mess up one stage and come to terms with it in the next. But as you start, a goal of some sort is essential.

You need to set out with some idea of the form you want to make,
be it spherical, tapered with legs, or a simple cylinder.

Painting your experimental forms black will allow you to study the shape without the grain and color of the wood intruding.

What you can do on a lathe is controlled by your tools and skill level. If you're a novice box turner or not completely at ease with the tools, try developing your ideas as solid forms on the lathe (see the bottom photo on the facing page). Use unattractive scraps, odd branches, or anything that allows you to work uninhibited by the fear of wasting good material. Then work out your forms and detailing while you find out exactly what you can do with your tools. Making solid forms is a great way to learn about both the tools and the design, and it can be an enormous help to those overly optimistic about their skills.

Keep everything you make so you can compare forms and determine why some are better or worse than others. You don't need to sand the forms, but spraying them black is a good idea because you can study them without being distracted by the grain and color of the wood (see the photo above).

Just remember, it pays to walk up some hills before tackling Mount Everest. Practice on a few plain and simple forms similar to the one in chapter 4 and get used to the steps and techniques involved before leaping into complicated designs. It will save a lot of heartache later, but not all (see my Graveyard on p. 151).

Practical Considerations

However eccentric the design, boxes are essentially containers and therefore practical objects that need to function. And since boxes come in

A paper-clip box needs a loose lid, which in this case is reversible to give you a change of scene.

A small V detail at the join makes prying the lid and base apart easier. Voamboana (front), Putumuju (rear); 1975; 2 in. (50mm) in diameter.

all shapes and sizes to hold all manner of things, it follows that there cannot be a definitive correct fit for the lid or a perfect form. Boxes can have bases from broad and flat to rounded; they can lie down or stand up.

FITTING THE LID

Imagine a box full of paper clips, with the lid on to keep the dust out. Then imagine yourself with a few sheets of paper nicely squared up in one hand, scrambling for a paper clip with the other hand. The paper-clip box needs a loose lid so you can get to the clips with your one free hand. Conversely, needle boxes rolling around in a sewing basket need tighter lids so they don't open, but not so tight that in the effort to get the lid off needles scatter far and wide. Or like pill boxes, a screw-on lid might be preferable as better protection against spilling.

I love boxes in which the lid, when you remove it, fits closely enough that there's a slight resistance from a vacuum. It's as if there's an elastic band somewhere inside trying to keep the lid on. But if, for various reasons, the lid becomes loose that is not necessarily a disaster: As we already know, there are times when loose lids are essential.

Rounded forms like these need a near-loose lid or a detail at the join that will allow you to pry the lid off. The finials on these forms aren't very strong and could break if they were used to pull the lid off. English oak; 1975; 2 in. (50mm) in diameter.

But no matter how snug the lid, it must be easy to remove. Woodturning is still a craft practiced mainly by men, often of strong grip, who know what it takes to get one of their lids off. But you need to assume that the guardian of your box is somewhat frail, possibly a trifle arthritic, hasn't been to the gym regularly for years, and is worried about damaging something while trying to get the lid off. I've encountered some amazingly tight lids over the years shown off by turners proud of the fit, but they are rarely practical except for funerary urns, when you generally want the lid to stay on. (Super Glue would make sure.)

There is a problem specific to rounded forms, where the join is on a tight curve (see the bottom photo on the facing page). The snag is that it is difficult to get a grip on the curved surfaces to pull them apart, so you need some detail at the join to slip a fingernail or knife into to pry the box open. On such forms turn at least a V at the join so the lid and base can be pried apart if need be (see the center photo on

If you detail the join between lid and base, you disguise any warping. These boxes, made in 1970, are Burmese teak, which is particularly stable, but the join on the plainer form is easy to feel now that the lid and base have moved in relation to one another. On the other box, the flamboyance of the lid totally disguises similar movement that has occurred.

Casuarina Box

Note that on either side of the join the form is almost cylindrical, making it easy to grip should the lid become tight. Spherical boxes with tight lids can be very hard to open, being very difficult to grasp, especially if highly polished.

MATERIAL:	Casuarina
SIZE:	3⅜ in. by 3⅜ in. (85mm by 85mm)

However eccentric the design, boxes are essentially containers and therefore practical objects that need to function.

Jewelry boxes are simpler to use when the lid comes off easily.

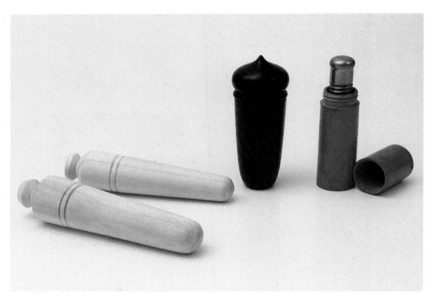

The dark box (center) falls over in a slight breeze. It has a threaded lid, but it might have been better with a rounded-over base like those on the needle cases (left), which aren't intended to stand upright. (Needle cases by Robert Schlange, Victor, Colorado.) The antique boxwood bottle container (right) has both a sensible base and the weight of the contents for stability.

p. 40). The other solution for rounded forms is to have a near-loose fit. You won't have this lid problem on straight-sided forms because you can get a firm grip on both the lid and base.

It was shortly after I started making Vs on rounded forms that I realized another benefit of detailing the join—it helped disguise the inevitable movement that occurs between the lid and base with humidity changes (see the photo at left on p. 41).

STABILIZING THE BOX

Another practical consideration is the stability of any box in relation to how it is likely to be used. One of the reasons all my early boxes had wide bases was because I imagined them in use as spice pots in kitchens. I aspired to selling large sets of boxes to fashion-conscious cooks, but I discovered that in fact most of the boxes seemed to end up on dressing tables storing jewelry. This is a more sedate occupation for a box, so gradually some curves crept in. Forms that are taller than they are wide need a broad foot or some weight in the base.

Aesthetics and Proportions

All over the world we find a consensus, which has bridged millennia, on which proportions are generally considered pleasing to the eye and which are not. In artifacts from ancient times, proportions that must have pleased ancient eyes are similar to those we admire in today's objects; only the details vary. Through the centuries, humans have invested vast amounts of time searching for mathematical formulae that will allow us to get proportions right every time. The Golden Rule, Fibonacci Series, and a Vedic formula each have ideal proportions in the region of 2:3 and 3:5, and these work well as overall dimensions for boxes, as does 3:4.

Of these well-proportioned boxes, the smallest is boxwood, made by Englishman Ray Key. The position of the join makes this box look taller than it is wide; in reality it's 1⅜ in. (35mm) square.

GENERIC FORMS FOR BOXES

A   B   C   D

A   B   C   D

A   B   C   D

A   B   C   D

When dividing a mass in two, it's good to have the parts uneven.

In A, the line is in the center, equidistant from the top and bottom, but the top half looks just slightly larger than the bottom. The overall form has a vaguely uncomfortable upward energy, which is unsettling in relation to some of the other forms.

In B, a line is added beneath the centerline, which accentuates this upward focus.

In C, a line is added above the centerline, and suddenly the form is less aggressive and appears more settled, lighter, and desirable. Of all of these forms, most people will find C the more appealing because the mass is divided into two uneven parts by the pair of lines, with the smaller portion on top.

In D, a third line is added at the top. I think it's one line too many, although it seems to work better in the rounded forms than the squared.

The yew box (left) looks hunched with the join line so high, whereas the similar form with a lower pair of grooves (right) looks more balanced.

Tower Series Boxes

These architecturally inspired forms look best clustered together. The tallest box unscrews in two places providing two storage areas in the one piece.

MATERIALS: Cocobolo and moose bone (small box in center) and Tasmanian blackwood (rest)

SIZES: 2 in. to 3 in. (50mm to 75mm) diameter

However, it is the way in which you subdivide that mass that often has greater visual impact and relevance in boxes because there will usually be a horizontal line dividing the primary mass. Where you place this line, in the form of the join between the lid and base, and how you manipulate detail around it greatly affects how your box will look (see the photos on p. 43 and above).

In the sets of generic forms in the drawings on p. 43 and the facing page, you can see how the placement of a line affects our perception of the form and how this can be manipulated by the addition of other lines.

Profiles

Curves must be considered when examining profiles. The major thing to remember about curves is that they curve: There should be no dips, bumps, or flat areas to mar the sweep of the bend. If the bend tightens, it should do so evenly, with no sudden changes in direction. There should be nothing to jar the senses as you fondle a curved surface. The best way to begin to appreciate the difference between good and not-so-good curves is to do a few prac-

BOXES DIVIDED IN THREE

In these forms, each mass is divided into three, and E is divided again. In A and B, the largest mass is in the center, but I prefer the symmetry of C, D, and E, with the portions evenly balanced.

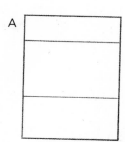

A

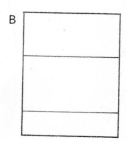

B

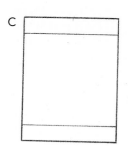

C

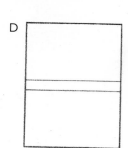

D

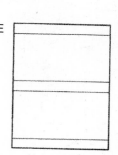

E

DOMED FORMS

In these domed forms, A has a hunched look and needs more detail to drag the eye down the form. The extra line in B does little to help move the eye downward. However, C, D, and E are more balanced, with the lines creating another substantial mass to break the starkness of the lower portion.

A

B

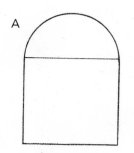

C

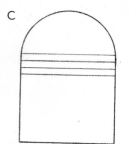

D

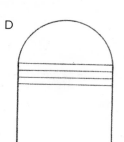

E

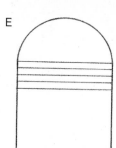

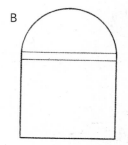

EXAMPLES OF PROFILE ASSESSMENT

Learning how to assess your profiles will help you make better-looking boxes.

1 The curves on these 2-in.- (50mm) diameter casuarina boxes are fine, but the detail, which is useful for separating contrasting curves, is fussy here. I was trying too hard.

2 Refined detailing separates contrasting curves on these cocobolo boxes. Note how the lower curves come inward slightly to the underside of the beads to contrast with the curve flowing out from the top bead.

3 Beware the dangers of being carried away by technique and no goal. The right box's profile is overburdened with ill-defined and unnecessary beads, which make the piece grossly top-heavy. The center lid is less cumbersome. The left box is better balanced, but still the lid is visually heavy.

4 These well-balanced forms made in 1989 have slightly convex sides to the base that lead the eye up toward the domes of the lids. They look good and feel much better than those in photo 3.

These boxes successfully incorporate curves that flow. Note in the center box that the curve flows under the beads, which might have been added afterward. The grooves on the left box are too deep and intrusive, especially when compared with those on the right box. Huon pine; 4¾ in. to 6 in. (120mm to 150mm) in diameter.

tice hollowings to cut in half (see the photo at right). If the curve doesn't flow, the fact will be immediately apparent in the cross section. I tend to use asymmetric curves and generally avoid circles and arcs, both generated by compasses, because they're a bit mechanical.

Beads and coves are useful for detailing the join and adjusting proportions. If you make a mess of turning them, don't worry: Replace them with grooves for the same visual effect. If you have three or more beads, stack them in order of size or keep them identical to look good. My usual practice is to have two beads and not worry about their being the same. I like the asymmetry, and my commercial bonus is that they are easier to do.

Finials and Knobs

So often the rounded top of a box looks bare and in need of a little something to finish things off. Is this urge to cap every dome some outward manifestation of a balding complex deeply seated within us? Lack of hair never worried me, but there is no doubt that a finial or a knob often seems to complete a design (see the top photos on p. 49).

This box felt so good and well balanced in my hand that I just had to cut it in half to try and find out why. In the cross section, we see that the curves flow nicely and the weight is evenly balanced between the lid and the base.

FINIALS AND KNOBS

Finials and knobs offer a chance to play with shapes. If you mess things up, you can always reduce a tall finial to a small knob.

A finial is just the right touch to complete the design of this domed box.

Tall finials and the more businesslike knobs are essentially handles to be grabbed, but this can be a problem on end-grain boxes. Because of the short grain in the lid, it doesn't take much force to break a knob free, leaving a hole in the top of the lid, which is fine if you always wanted a box for string—not something most of us want. To help prevent breakage, you can design the inside of the lid to be thicker at the base of the finial (see the drawing on p. 50). In 1975, I gave up putting either finials or knobs on the boxes I sold through American outlets because of manufacturer's liability insurance. First my broker demanded a truly staggering premium, then decided he wouldn't insure my boxes at all. The argument was that the finials were fragile, which was true, and that a child might possibly break one off, swallow it, and die.

In place of long and spiky finials and knobs I have used compact unbreakable and ungraspable beads and knobettes to crown my lids. I enjoy

Finials like this are easily broken free, leaving a hole in the lid if it is left too thin. However, the natural inclination of most people on a box of this scale is to grasp the lid on the fullest diameter, just above the bead, so breakage isn't normally a problem. Yew; 1975; 1⅜ in. (35mm) in diameter.

VARIATIONS FOR LID INSIDES

To retain some strength without making the lid too bulky, make sure there's ample wood at the base of the finial. As you can see, I like to decorate the inside of the lid while retaining the bulk.

The amount of wood beneath the bead on the left lid below is about right. The amount on the similar right lid, however, is too short and will break easily if any kind of force is applied.

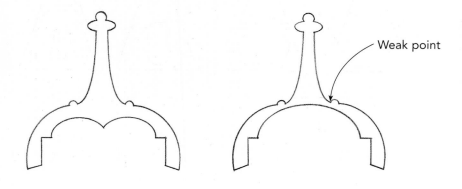

Weak point

the finesse required when turning these, and I use a ⅜-in. (10mm) gouge almost exclusively for the task. With these compact types, as with any sort of finial or knob, you need to incorporate some thicker areas to take the strain. Much as nature has done with our bodies' bones, you need to work out where the greatest stress is likely to be and design accordingly.

The Inside

One of the exciting things about opening a box is that you never know for sure what the inside will reveal. Like those pyramids built in ancient Egypt, a great mass might contain very little but make a striking statement (see the drawing below).

A superb Japanese box with an inner lid, which fits as perfectly as the main lid. Elm; 3 in. (75mm) in diameter.

DISTRIBUTING WEIGHT WITHIN A GIVEN FORM

These forms offer four different insides within the same basic cone. Note how the horizontal line of the join changes our perception of the overall shape. Since most people expect the inside form to echo the profile, A's thin and even wall is fairly predictable, but the others are likely to surprise. B has a lid within the lid, as has D. The weight of C is bound to be unexpected because the opening inside is so small compared with the size of the whole box, but it would function well for small earrings or studs. D is designed specifically for earrings.

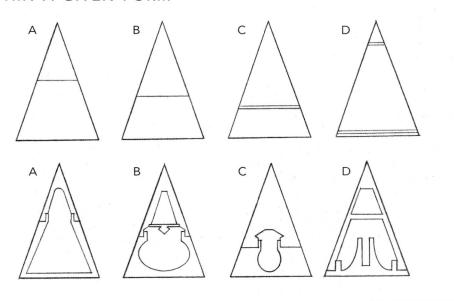

Much as nature has done with our bodies' bones, you need to work out where the greatest stress is likely to be and design accordingly.

WALL THICKNESS AND DISTRIBUTED WEIGHT

In A, we see a common wall thickness, with the base hollowed straight in, leaving a thickish wall. If the inside is dovetailed as in B, all the weight is in the top of the box and doesn't feel right. C keeps the weight better distributed between top and bottom.

A

B

C

Bottoms should be turned slightly concave so the box sits flat on the rim.

Even within a very simple thin-walled box, you must pay particular attention to the wall thickness, especially in the top and bottom. If either is left too thick, the physical balance will be upset so the piece won't feel good in the hand (see the drawing on the facing page).

The Bottom

Time was when my technical skills were so suspect and my cash flow so poor that I never risked turning the bottoms of any of my boxes; I just put them to a sander. The bottom was flat, the rim sharp, and when (frequently) I failed to keep the base at 90° to the axis, the boxes had a lean. I wasn't near enough Pisa to cash in, so eventually I had to learn to turn off the bases to eliminate the leans. As I developed confidence, I started putting grooves on the concave bottoms, just to show up the competition, who did not.

If you want your box to sit square on a surface rather than spin on a convex bottom like a deformed spinning top, the base needs to be finished nicely and should be slightly concave.

Once you get into the routine of making boxes and don't have to think too much about what to do next at any given stage, there should be enough leeway to keep you occupied discovering the myriad outside/inside combinations. Hopefully, this has been a chapter that has alerted you to some possibilities. If you have never made a box, or only a few, I urge you to work through the next chapter a few times, referring to chapter 5 (on lids) as your skills develop.

Mosque Boxes

Note how the vertical sides are slightly curved and tapered. The bends and chamfers are used to relieve otherwise stock forms and widen the bases.

MATERIALS:	Cocobolo (left and right) and bacote (center)
SIZES:	2 in. (50mm) and 1¾ in. (45mm) diameter

4 MAKING AN END-GRAIN BOX

Making an end-grain box is a challenging exercise, but it's worth the effort when the result is a good-looking container with the grain running from top to bottom and a snug-fitting lid. Success comes from following the routine assiduously. In this chapter, I'll detail the steps for making the end-grain box in the photo on p. 71, including any problems or things to look out for. You can follow these steps to make this particular box, or you can modify them slightly to make a similar one of your own. Once you've learned the routine, you'll find that your enjoyment of this aspect of turning wood increases no end.

Making this box is easy enough if you proceed cautiously. You must pay attention to the warnings and follow the steps in order if you want to be successful. I say this to every group of students I have for my hands-on workshops, but we do well if we get even 2 half-decent boxes from the first 20 attempts. Most novices tend to forge ahead over seemingly little points, like steps 3, 4, and 9, only to discover later that they need to start over.

You need to have a reasonable idea of what you want to make at the outset. Boxes are made from the inside out, so we'll start with the inside of the lid, then complete the inside of the base. Once the inside is done, you put the lid and the base together and turn the profile as a whole, rechucking the base in order to turn the bottom.

Try not to be too nervous about the tools. I know a lot of inexperienced turners are pretty terrified of the skew chisel, but most of the worst catches occur using scrapers—often a favored tool. Now is the time to practice and hone your skills, especially with the tools you find more difficult. Then, when you need to produce a first-class box, you can proceed, confident of success.

For this box, you'll need to prepare a cylindrical blank about 3 in. (75mm) in diameter and 5 in. (125mm) long (see "Preparing Blanks" on p. 32). Before you begin turning, it's a good idea to study the full-scale cross-section view of the box. (See the drawing on the facing page. You might want to photocopy this drawing and p. 71 and pin them near the lathe for when you turn.)

CROSS SECTION OF AN END-GRAIN BOX

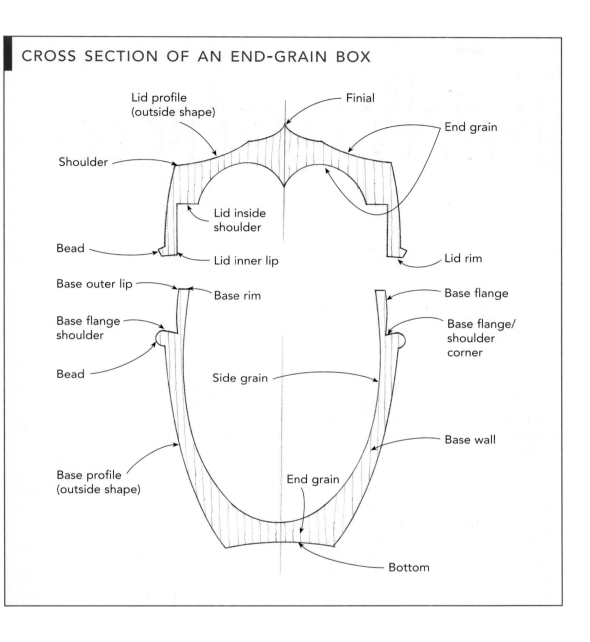

Lid profile (outside shape)

Finial

End grain

Shoulder

Lid inside shoulder

Bead

Lid inner lip

Lid rim

Base outer lip

Base rim

Base flange

Base flange shoulder

Base flange/ shoulder corner

Bead

Side grain

Base wall

Base profile (outside shape)

End grain

Bottom

Boxes are made from the inside out.

Step 1: Start by mounting the lid section with the top in the chuck jaws. Locating the top should be easy if you have shoulders turned on either end of your blank (see the drawing at right below). Ensure that the wood is properly in the chuck, with either the shoulder on the blank hard against the chuck jaws or with the flat end of the blank seated on the base of the jaws. End-grain blanks don't warp much, so if the blank is wildly off-center when you turn on the lathe, stop the machine and check to make sure the wood is seated properly.

True the blank (see the photos on p. 58). Get into the habit of truing any job on the lathe so that you get rid of everything you don't want early on. Stop the lathe occasionally to check, or you might discover some split or other defect when the job is almost finished. Common errors include leaving a flat remnant of the squared blank and forgetting about the end grain entirely or failing to get it cut clean enough. The end grain is important. It needs to be chamfered inward a few degrees because it's going to be the rim that sits on the base-flange shoulder. If it isn't true, it won't sit flat. If you neglect the chamfer, the join between lid and base can look terrible.

I use a skew chisel rather than a gouge to smooth the cylinder so I can see how the wood works and if twisted grain will pluck out (see photo 1b on p. 58). If it does pluck out, it

CUTTING SEQUENCE FOR A LID

The step numbers appear in parentheses.
Cut 1: Chamfer the rim with the skew chisel long point (step 1).

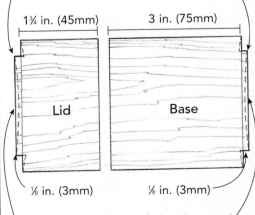

Cuts 2–4: Back-hollow away from center with a gouge (step 2) or cuts 2–6: hollow toward center with a gouge (step 2).

Cuts 7 and 8: Cut the flange with a square-end scraper (step 3).
Cut 9: Finish the end grain with a roundnose scraper (step 5).
Cuts 10 and 11: Begin the profile (step 8).

PREPARED BLANK FOR AN END-GRAIN BOX

Turn shoulders flat or slightly concave.

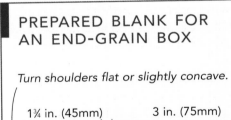

1¾ in. (45mm) — Lid
3 in. (75mm) — Base
⅛ in. (3mm)
⅛ in. (3mm)

End grain turned true, defect free, and slightly concave

Warning: Do not attempt to separate the lid and base sections using a power saw. Use a parting tool on the lathe.

warns me to be extra cautious come the final shaping of the profile.

Step 2: Roughly hollow the lid (see the drawing at left on the facing page). I use a ½-in. (15mm) shallow or half-round gouge with fingernail grind.

Step 3: Cut the flange at least ½ in. (15mm) deep (see photo 3 on p. 58). This is the portion of the lid that fits over the base flange. The flange must be cylindrical, which means the sides must be parallel. This is the first place things can really go wrong. If you don't cut this flange as a cylinder, you'll have all sorts of problems when you come to jam it over the base in order to complete the outside, and you'll never get a suction fit to your lid. (There's more about flanges on pp. 73–76.)

I use a square-end scraper to make this cut. Make sure the tool rest is at center height or just above (see the drawing on p. 59). If the rest is too low, the scraper is eased right as the cut proceeds because the lower side of the tool rides against the rim of the flange. If you roll the tool so the top left corner can cut, you risk a big catch on the end grain.

Do not use a skew chisel to cut the flange! The tool sides keep the point away from the line you need to cut and drift it right as you cut. If you tilt the skew chisel upward, the same thing happens, and you increase the severity of any catch.

Step 4: Check that you have turned a cylinder. This is very important. Use internal spring calipers with an adjustment wheel to do this, taking three deliberate steps. Start by squeezing the calipers together, then release them at the bottom of the flange on the maximum diameter. Adjust the wheel until you can feel the spring pressure against it. Finally, pull the calipers to the opening. Ideally, you will feel the sides brushing the points evenly all the way to the rim.

Inset Dome Box

Note how a frame for the fan pattern on the top is created by recessing the dome. The decorative beads at the rim of the lid and the box add visual interest.

MATERIAL:	Laburnum
SIZE:	2¾ in. by 2 in. (70mm by 50mm)

CUTTING THE LID FLANGE

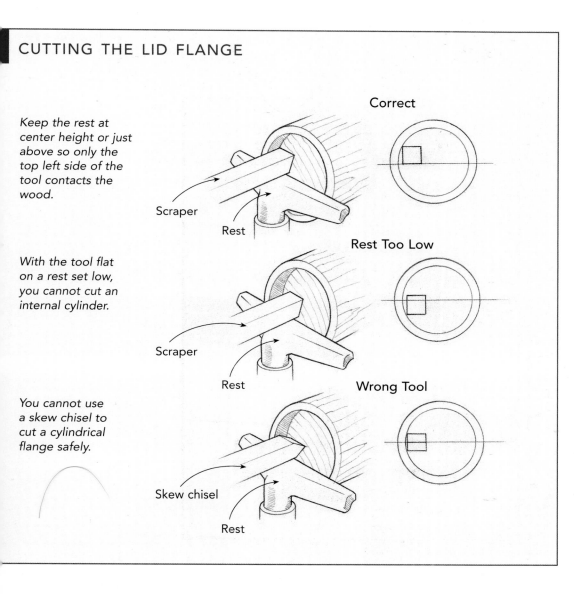

Keep the rest at center height or just above so only the top left side of the tool contacts the wood.

Scraper

Rest

Correct

With the tool flat on a rest set low, you cannot cut an internal cylinder.

Scraper

Rest

Rest Too Low

You cannot use a skew chisel to cut a cylindrical flange safely.

Skew chisel

Rest

Wrong Tool

Mostly you won't have a cylinder, so you need to establish what needs to be turned away to make one. If you pull the calipers out easily and the points don't span the gap at the rim, you need to cut a wedge from the rim to the base of the flange. If you cannot remove the calipers without squeezing them in, you have a dovetail. So squeeze the calipers to remove them, then release them at the rim and see how much you need to turn away to get back to the

cylinder. This is a common situation that demands the spring calipers.

Refine the lid flange as required. It pays to take the time to get this right. Watch the progress of your cut on the far side of center (the lower right as you look at the end grain).

Step 5: Finish turning the inside of the lid using a round-nose scraper. I leave a small shoulder between the flange and the end grain. These

two areas are finished differently, with the flange hardly sanded and the end grain often needing quite a lot. Thus there will be a different surface quality to each area. The shoulder defines the boundary. (There is more about this in "Inside the Lid" on p. 87.)

Step 6: True the rim. The lid will change shape slightly because as the inside is removed, the stresses are altered. Check that the rim is chamfered with the inner lip lower than the outer. This cut is made using a skew chisel flat on the rest as a scraper. The advantage over a scraper is that the tool is skewed, so it is difficult to put very much pressure against the end grain. Keep your hand firmly on the rest and squeeze the tool into the end grain. Don't push it forward across the rest.

Step 7: Sand and polish the inside of the lid. Use cloth-backed abrasives and your choice of polish. Keep sanding to a minimum on the flange. A light touch with 240 grit followed by 400 grit should be sufficient to smooth the sur-

face without distorting the cylinder. Take care not to sand the inner lip of the rim. One safety note: Never wrap the polishing cloth around your fingers.

Step 8: Begin shaping the lid profile. You do this now because the lid is held in a chuck. If you leave it until later, the lid will be jammed on the base and much less secure. So while it may not seem you are achieving much, it's a heck of a lot easier than leaving it until later. Start to detail the lid/base join by putting a small chamfer on the rim. I use a small gouge for shaping and the long point of a skew chisel for the end-grain chamfer.

Step 9: Mount the base section as you did the lid in step 1 and establish the approximate diameter of the base flange. Use the skew chisel to peel a tapered flange so the lid just fits over the end. Hold the lid lightly to the flange so you get a slight burnish. This gives you the exact lid diameter. *Do not fit the lid on tight now!* This is the stage where things go wrong. The idea is to

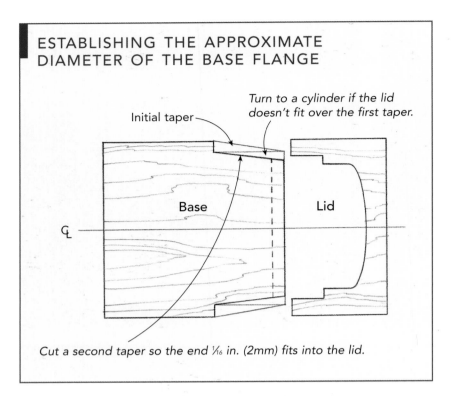

ESTABLISHING THE APPROXIMATE DIAMETER OF THE BASE FLANGE

Initial taper

Turn to a cylinder if the lid doesn't fit over the first taper.

Base

Lid

℄

Cut a second taper so the end ¹⁄₁₆ in. (2mm) fits into the lid.

off-center. You can recover from this by cutting back into the base.

Don't mess with calipers at this stage. Gauge the diameter of the flange by eye. It's good practice and helps develop your eye's sense of proportion. You can see pretty well how much you need to remove when you hold the lid up to the end grain. If the lid won't fit over the flange on the first attempt, reduce the taper to a cylinder at the diameter of the rim (see the drawing at left). Then create another taper over which the lid will fit, or repeat the cycle with another cylinder. This gives you a known starting point for the next cut. If you only reduce the diameter of the taper, you don't know, as the cut proceeds, where you started. Consequently, it's very easy to turn too small a taper. If you do turn too small a taper, trim away some of the end grain and work back into the body of the blank. This is one of the advantages of overfitting lids: You have a margin for error.

Step 10: Shape the inside (see the drawing on p. 64). Ensure that the inside either is cylindrical or widens from the rim so that the base is easy to rechuck when it's time to finish the bottom. Use gouges to rough-hollow and scrapers to finish. Keep your weight over the handle to control small catches.

If you have a catch that pulls the wood off-center or even out of the chuck, don't worry. Just pop it back as near true as possible and carry on. If you've already fitted the lid tight, though, you've got problems. You might manage an accurate rechucking, but generally you'll have to go back to step 9 to re-turn the flange as instructed. If that's not possible, you'll need to start the whole thing again—a new lid from a new blank—if you want to end up with a halfdecent box.

Step 11: Measure and mark the exact internal depth on the outside of the base. You need to know the exact depth if you are to control the thickness of the base precisely.

establish the approximate diameter of the flange over which the lid will fit, then complete the internal shaping and finishing before the outside is shaped. This is done for a couple of reasons.

First, if you fail to fit the lid roughly and establish the approximate diameter of the flange, you can easily remove so much from the center that there's nothing left to fit the lid on. I've seen lids that fit right inside, and it's not what you want.

Second, if you fit the lid on tight at this stage then hollow the inside, chances are that in the end the lid will be off-center or loose. As you finish the inside, the base is likely to go slightly oval as stresses alter with the removal of wood or with frictional heat as you sand and polish. You will then need to true the flange, and that will loosen the lid. Or you could have a catch that moves the base off-center. Again, after you true the flange the lid will be loose or

Ensure that the inside either is cylindrical or widens from the rim so that the base is easy to rechuck when it's time to finish the bottom.

CUTTING SEQUENCE FOR A BASE

The step numbers appear in parentheses.

Cut 1: Establish approximate diameter of the flange with a skew chisel (step 9).

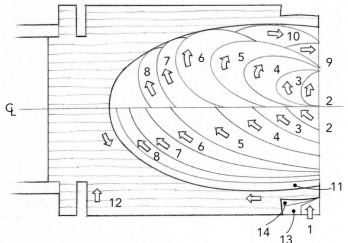

Cuts 2–10 (top half): Back-hollow away
from center with a gouge (step 10)
or cuts 2–8 (bottom half): hollow toward center with a gouge (step 10).
Cut 11: Refine the surface with a scraper (step 10).
Cut 12: Begin parting with a parting tool (step 12).
Cuts 13 and 14: Fit the lid tight with a skew chisel (step 14).

Step 12: Part in immediately to the headstock side of the depth line. The idea is to establish exactly the inside depth and then to keep track of it. For this box, I know that the bottom of the inside of the box is one tool width away from the left side of the parting cut, so I must maintain that shoulder until I am ready to part off the box.

Step 13: Sand and polish the inside of the base.

Step 14: Refine the base flange and fit the lid on tight (see the photos on the facing page). One of the reasons you spent time getting the flange cylindrical in steps 3 and 4 is so you can jam the lid easily on the base flange, which

should now be turned to a barely discernible taper of about 1°. This is a tricky stage. If you push the lid over the flange with too steep a taper, you can split the lid. If the lid is loose, you'll have problems shaping the lid profile because the lid won't stay on.

Start by truing the base flange again, then hold the lid over the end to get a fresh burnish mark. Where the lid rubs it fits. Use a skew chisel flat on the rest for an ultralight peel/scrape cut, taking very little dustlike shavings. Fit the lid in two stages. (At the start you should have a base flange as in the drawing on p. 66.)

First, reduce the diameter to the burnish mark you just made. When the lid fits on tightly, extend the flange to the required depth and chamfer the base-flange shoulder so the rim is the highest point (see the drawing on p. 66). If the lid is barely on tightly and spins as you work it, remove the lid and, with the lathe still running, hold a lump of pure beeswax against the base flange to build a layer of wax. Then stop the lathe and quickly push the lid on before the wax hardens. This should keep the lid on, but if not, build up a thicker layer of wax. Eventually, after the profile is shaped all you will need to do is hold the lid as the base spins, melting the wax and probably leaving you with a satisfactory lid fit.

Step 15: Roughly shape the profile, establishing overall proportions (see the drawing on p. 68). I use a gouge for this. At this stage, I rarely risk a skew-chisel shear cut in case some grain lifts around the thinner sections over the flanges.

Step 16: Detail the join with the long point of a skew chisel so that the inevitable movement between the lid and base is disguised. Go for the beads, but don't worry if you make a mess of them at first. Just turn them away and cut a little chamfer on the shoulders of both the rim and the base to create a V groove.

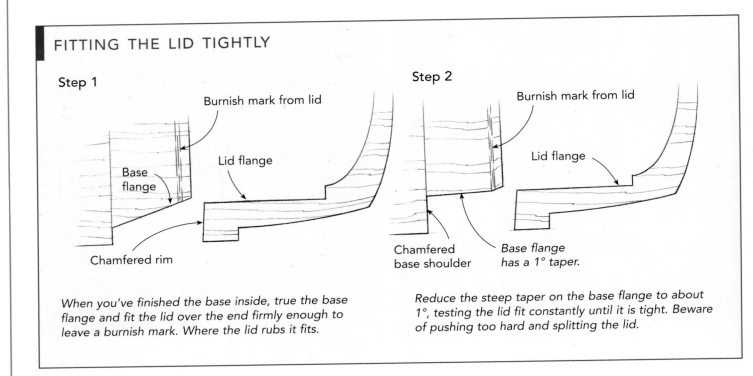

FITTING THE LID TIGHTLY

Step 1

Burnish mark from lid

Base flange

Lid flange

Chamfered rim

When you've finished the base inside, true the base flange and fit the lid over the end firmly enough to leave a burnish mark. Where the lid rubs it fits.

Step 2

Burnish mark from lid

Lid flange

Chamfered base shoulder

Base flange has a 1° taper.

Reduce the steep taper on the base flange to about 1°, testing the lid fit constantly until it is tight. Beware of pushing too hard and splitting the lid.

In earlier stages, you chamfered the lid rim and base-flange shoulder. As you cut on the join, a gap will open because of the chamfers, and this helps you gauge the exact wall thickness of the lid. Chamfer each rim before pushing the lid on tight. If you can't push the lid on, the base flange is too long and needs shortening. Very small amounts are easily sanded away, but anything over ⅟₃₂ in. (1mm) will have to be turned, and this can cause the inner lip to splinter away.

If you need to turn the rim off the flange, cut a small V groove just in from the end so that when the skew point cuts the innermost fibers there will be minimal splitting and damage to the new inner lip, which can then be easily sanded smooth. (See the drawing on p. 77.)

Step 17: Refine the profile but retain the headstock side of the parting cut. This is your point of reference for the internal depth of the base, which you know is one tool width away. Having used a small gouge to rough the overall form, now it's time to attend to the detail. Use a skew chisel to make a peel/scrape cut: The grain is unlikely to be absolutely straight and might pick out if you use standard skew-chisel techniques in tight areas. I find the peel/scrape cut the most effective because although the surface is not as smooth as with a shear cut, it is very controlled and requires little sanding.

Step 18: Sand and polish the profile.

Step 19: Fine-fit the lid. This is a step often forgotten now that the end of the project is in sight. It can be done later, but now is much easier. Try to avoid using abrasives because their use will tend to make the flange oval and thus affect the quality of the lid fit. The best method is an ultradelicate peel/scrape cut with a skew chisel. Take a very light cut, barely touching the flange, to remove any slight eccentricity, then

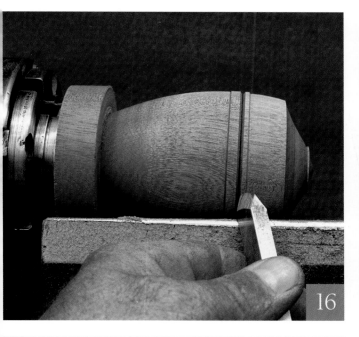

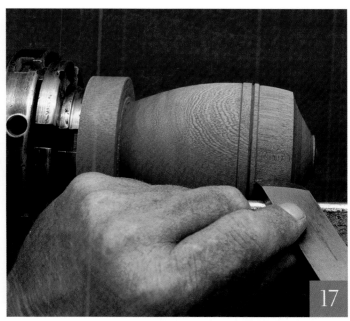

PROFILE CUTS

The step numbers appear in parentheses.

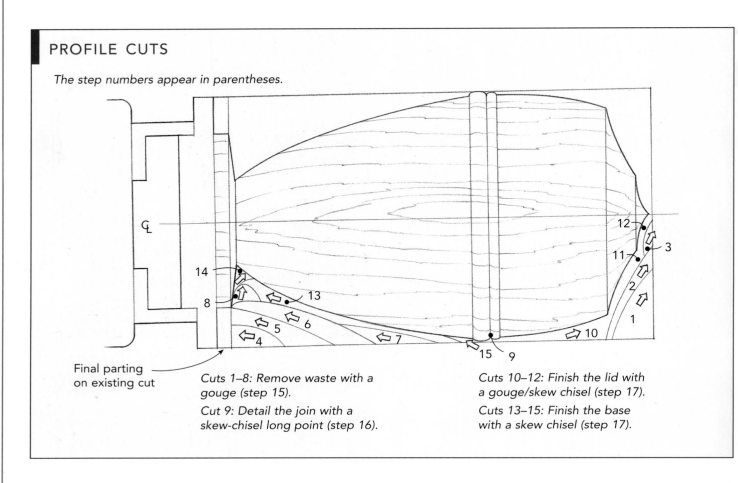

Final parting on existing cut

Cuts 1–8: Remove waste with a gouge (step 15).

Cut 9: Detail the join with a skew-chisel long point (step 16).

Cuts 10–12: Finish the lid with a gouge/skew chisel (step 17).

Cuts 13–15: Finish the base with a skew chisel (step 17).

hold the lid over the flange to create another burnish mark. If the lid isn't held absolutely square you will have two separate lines or one broad one. Reduce the diameter to the center of the line(s), stop the lathe, and test the lid.

If the base flange is still somewhat tapered, you will feel increasing resistance the farther on the lid goes and will need to take more very light cuts until the lid slides on and off easily. Cut in a fraction as you near the base flange/shoulder corner so the flange becomes slightly curved, but don't remove the burnish mark. (For more on fitting the lid see chapter 5.)

Step 20: Polish the flange. I occasionally use some 240-grit or finer abrasive to soften the flange first, but I aim to cut it clean enough that this isn't required.

Step 21: Part off the base. The headstock side of the parting cut made earlier remains, showing you that the inside is a parting-tool width away. By aligning the right side of the parting tool with the edge of the earlier parting cut, you know the thickness of the box base equals the width of the parting tool. One tip: Catch the base—don't hold it. Otherwise you risk the fibers being torn from the base of the box.

Step 22: Rechuck the base the same way you chucked the lid over the base. Ensure that the base rim abuts a shoulder or, as in this case, the chuck jaws. Use a skew chisel flat on the rest to make a peel/scrape cut. In photo 22 on the facing page, I was almost out of wood with no margin for error.

Step 23: Finish turning the base with a small gouge or small skew chisel. The small gouge has more bevel to ride on the end grain as the cut proceeds, allowing more control in the not-infrequent event of the base coming loose. It pays to have a hand over the base to prevent it from flying.

Ensure the bottom is concave, using the gouge as a convenient straightedge, unless you want a rocking or spinning box. (Tool junkies will no doubt have a special box-bottom concavity-measuring device, and if one doesn't exist, there's clearly an opening in the market and a fortune to be made.)

Step 24: Refine the profile as it curves into the base (see photo 24 above left). A skew chisel will give the best finish here, as the cut is across the grain. I refine the curve after turning the base so that I eliminate the burnish mark often associated with the beginning of a cut across end grain.

Step 25: Sand and polish the base.

If you forgot to fine-fit the lid earlier, or if the lid has tightened after the box was completed, you will need to rechuck the base to refine the flange. Just rechuck as you did to finish the bottom and work on the flange. The tedious bit is having to remove the base every few seconds to check how the fit is going, but it's worth the effort.

A STEP-BY-STEP GUIDE TO TURNING END-GRAIN BOXES

1. Mount the lid blank and turn it true. Chamfer the end grain until it's slightly concave. (Skew chisel)

2. Rough-hollow the lid. (Gouge)

3. Cut the lid flange. (Square-end scraper)

4. Check that the flange is cylindrical and refine as required. (Calipers)

5. Finish turning the inside of the lid. (Round-nose scraper)

6. True the lid rim. (Skew chisel as a scraper)

7. Sand and polish the inside of the lid.

8. Begin shaping the outside of the lid. (Gouge and skew chisel)

9. Mount the base blank and establish the approximate diameter of the base flange. *Don't fit the lid now!* (Skew chisel for peeling)

10. Shape the inside. (Gouge and scrapers)

11. Mark the exact internal depth.

12. Part to the headstock side of the internal depth line. (Parting tool)

13. Sand and polish the inside of the base.

14. Refine the flange and fit the lid on tight. (Skew chisel for peel/scrape)

15. Roughly shape the profile. (Gouge)

16. Detail the join and refine the profile. (Skew chisel)

17. Finish turning the profile. Retain the headstock side of the parting cut. (Skew chisel)

18. Sand and polish the profile.

19. Fine-fit the lid. (Skew chisel for peel/scrape)

20. Polish the flange.

21. Part off the base. (Parting tool)

22. Rechuck the base. (Skew chisel)

23. Turn the bottom to make it concave and check it with a straightedge. (Gouge or skew chisel)

24. Refine the profile curve near the base. (Skew chisel)

25. Sand and polish the base.

The finished end-grain box.

5 MORE ABOUT LIDS

For me, the attraction and challenge of turning boxes lies in creating a lid that pulls off with a soft plop as the air rushes in to fill the vacuum. I love the feel of that slight pull from within. In the late '70s, I reckoned that as I lifted a box by the lid the base should be carried up by a slight vacuum, only to drop free when scarcely in the air. Now I like lids a shade tighter than that.

It's a tricky thing to get right every time because I want the lid to come off easily but not fall off if the box is held upside down by the base. Getting this right continues to be a challenge and ongoing source of satisfaction.

Lids can be made to fit either in or over a base, but I have always made over-fitting lids because they allow a greater margin for error and are more practical. In-fitting lids can be very quick to turn, so they are often the favored method of capping a cylinder, in a rough-and-ready sort of a way, to create a very cheap box. Aesthetically they look fine, but my main gripe against them is that the flange occupies storage space in the base.

Some years ago in Cornwall, England, I encountered a shallow box where the in-fitting lid barely left room for a couple of postage stamps. Possibly the guy who made it had a problem keeping his stamps flat in the damp winters, but to me it was an extreme example of the major disadvantage of the in-fitting lid. The major advantage is that the base can be designed as a piece in its own right, to survive, if need be, a lost or broken lid.

If an in-fitting lid binds or jams, it can be almost impossible to remove without breaking unless it is thick and has a solid knob. Unfortunately, the solidity (and consequent weight) necessary to support a suitable knob makes for a pretty unattractive lid. I consider in-fitting lids more suited to larger pieces and a loose fit. The typical short flange on an in-fitting lid demands extreme finesse with the tools, since the slightest catch pulls the lid free of any jam fit. Because of this, I tend to make the lid separately from the base, mounting it over a chuck. On boxes up to 3 in. (75mm) it's just as easy to make an in-fitting suction-fit lid with nice detail on both sides as it is to make an over-fitting lid, but there is less margin for error.

In the final analysis, an in-fitting lid tends to demand more of you, while returning less.

A loose lid is generally preferable for a large-diameter form. Barrel form; 1996; 4¾ in. (120mm) in diameter.

By contrast, the over-fitting lid doesn't occupy valuable storage space created in the base. A long flange is easy to accommodate within most designs without adversely affecting the form. Rather, it enables you to create a more desirable fit and a lid that is more secure when jammed over the base for the crucial shaping of the profile. If you make a mess of the base flange, you can cut back into the base and rescue the situation fairly easily. You might have to alter your design and ideas somewhat, but that's often how you come to explore new shapes. In the final analysis, an in-fitting lid tends to demand more of you, while returning less.

Suction-Fit Lids

Suction-fit lids require a more detailed explanation than they received in chapter 4. Achieving a soft suction fit is rather like climbing a mountain: You come over a rise expecting to see the summit only to discover there's another rise to go. You might think you have the fit, but adjust the flanges and you'll often find an improvement. You'll have to lose a few boxes in the learning process, but I think it's worth the effort. There are flange combinations that work adequately, and, of course, some that don't. Here I'll look at how and where things go wrong

The wide burnish mark on the very shallow taper of the flange indicates exactly where the lid fits.

Now take a very light peeling/scrape cut from the left side of the burnish mark toward the base of the flange (see the photo at left). Use a skew chisel ground with a slightly curved edge. Keep the tool flat on the rest and use only the first ⅛ in. (3mm) of the long point to reduce the diameter of the flange on the base-shoulder side of the burnish mark to a cylinder. You need to keep most of the burnish mark because this is the exact diameter of the lid. You cannot measure more accurately, so you don't need calipers. Use the side of the bevel as a scraper to refine the base shoulder.

At this stage you might want to opt for a cylindrical base flange, which will fit into the lid like a piston into a cylinder (see the center drawing on the facing page). If the fit is really good, you can have a problem getting the lid on because of air pressure building inside. And if you eventually get the lid on, it might be quite difficult to get off again because of the suction. For lids like this with flanges 1 in. to 1⅜ in. (25mm to 35mm) long, you can run a small rounded point or inkless ballpoint pen along a line of grain to create a vent channel to release the pressure. By sanding the flanges very lightly, it is possible to arrive at a very soft piston effect. However, it is very easy to overdo it and end up with a loose fit, particularly if you are not familiar with the characteristics of your wood.

I prefer the base flange turned to a very slight curve, the crown of which fits into the cylindrical lid flange. You get this effect by testing the lid at least once along the way. When you have the base flange cylindrical and the lid eases on with some pressure resistance, further reduce the diameter of the flange against the shoulder, creating a slight curve (see the bottom drawing on the facing page). You will find that the lid pushes on more easily with this done. With some woods—particularly ash, maple, and walnut—if you push the lid on too forcefully when testing the fit with the lathe running, the friction will burn a line. The line is almost decorative, although not quite, and the technique

so that you can avoid problems when you make this type of lid.

A long flange is a great start to a suction fit, which is basically a piston where one cylinder (the lid) slides over another (the base). I like a minimum of ⅜ in. (10mm) of contact between the lid and base flanges, not only for the suction but also because I reckon this to be about the minimum for chucking the lid over the base securely. You can manage with less, but the slightest catch will cause the lid to fly off.

When it's time to fine-fit the lid (see step 19 on p. 66), you should have the box nearly finished, with a cylindrical flange in the lid that you took pains to get right earlier (see steps 3 and 4 on p. 57). At this stage, although the lid jams over the base, if you hold it lightly over the rotating base flange (see the top drawing on the facing page), it will rub and leave a burnished line about halfway along the flange. This can be two lines if you don't hold the lid absolutely square.

DIFFERENT TYPES OF LID FIT

Measuring the exact diameter

Hold the lid over the base just firmly enough to burnish the flange. This mark identifies the exact diameter on which the lid fits.

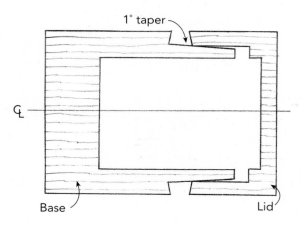

1° taper

C̵L

Base

Lid

Piston fit

For this fit, a cylindrical lid flange goes over a cylindrical base flange.

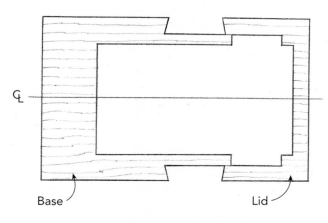

C̵L

Base

Lid

Suction fit

For this fit, a cylindrical lid flange goes over a curved base flange.

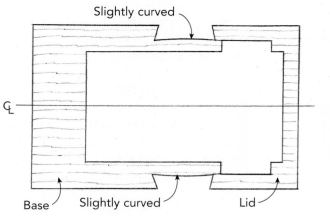

Slightly curved

C̵L

Base

Slightly curved

Lid

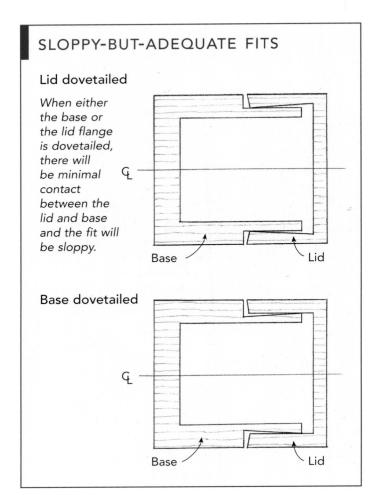

SLOPPY-BUT-ADEQUATE FITS

Lid dovetailed

When either the base or the lid flange is dovetailed, there will be minimal contact between the lid and base and the fit will be sloppy.

Base   Lid

Base dovetailed

Base   Lid

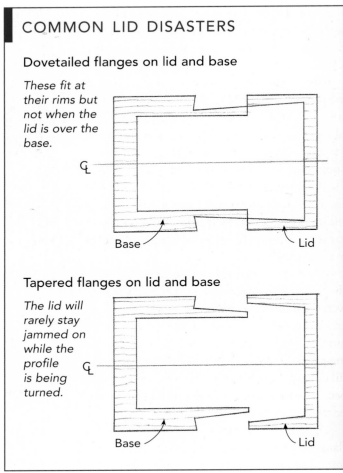

COMMON LID DISASTERS

Dovetailed flanges on lid and base

These fit at their rims but not when the lid is over the base.

Base   Lid

Tapered flanges on lid and base

The lid will rarely stay jammed on while the profile is being turned.

Base   Lid

fits the lid instantly, leaving little to do except apply the polish. Any sanding will make the lid loose.

During this process there will be several occasions when the novice will think: Wow! I've succeeded!—or something along those lines. The fit is rarely as good as it could be. The difference between the adequate and the excellent is enormous, and the only way you're going to find out is by messing up a few times. At some stage, as with everything in life, you have to experience the parameters for yourself. I can't tell you what they are any more than I can tell you what a weight feels like: The word heavy is not sufficient to describe the sensation. But

regarding lids, there are some pointers for how to improve fit.

If the lid needs a final push to snap its rim against the base shoulder, the base flange is still thickening toward the base of the shoulder. You need to get the skew point right into the corner. This thickening at the base of the base flange will also cause the lid to spring off the shoulder as you remove it, as if it's spring-loaded. It may seem pretty subtle, but getting rid of that little bit in the corner makes all the difference.

If the suction needs reducing to enable you to get the lid on and off more easily, a dab with 240 grit on the crown of the base flange should be sufficient to free it up.

The end of the base flange will probably taper slightly, but if it doesn't, sand a small chamfer on the outer lip of the base rim so that it locates easily into the lid.

It all seems so easy you might wonder where the problems arise. Most difficulties stem from failing to cut a cylindrical flange into the lid (see steps 3 and 4 on p. 57), so you are left with either a taper or a dovetail. If either flange is dovetailed, there is minimal contact between the two flanges, so the fit is essentially sloppy and never feels quite right (see the drawing at left on the facing page). Flanges like this make turning the lid profile more difficult and catches more dramatic.

While roughing the profile or rechucking the base, you may run into a problem. If the lid won't jam on because both lid and base flanges are dovetailed, you won't be able to turn the outside (see the drawing above right on the facing page). You may be tempted to use paper to fill the gap, but that won't help the end product because you'll have a very sloppy lid that might be tough to get on.

The solution is to reduce the length of the flange (see the drawing at right), then cut back into the shoulder of the base, turning a short section to fit the lid. When shortening the flange, it is easy to split away the fibers on the inner lip. Avoid this by using the long point of a skew chisel to cut a small V groove near the end of the flange. As the skew point breaks through, the length of grain on either side limits splintering on the innermost fibers. Chances are that you'll be left with a sort of groove in the old corner (see the drawing at right). Make this a proper groove, and maybe put in another, too, so you have a decorative feature on the flange (see the photo at right above).

Another common but near-hopeless situation you tend to discover when you're roughing the profile, after you have established the diameter of the base flange, is that the lid will not stay on easily—if at all—even if your tapered surfaces match (see the bottom right drawing

After you've shortened the flange, you may end up with a leftover groove from the old corner. Turn this groove into a decorative element by adding another groove near it.

REDUCING FLANGE TO CORRECT A SLOPPY FIT

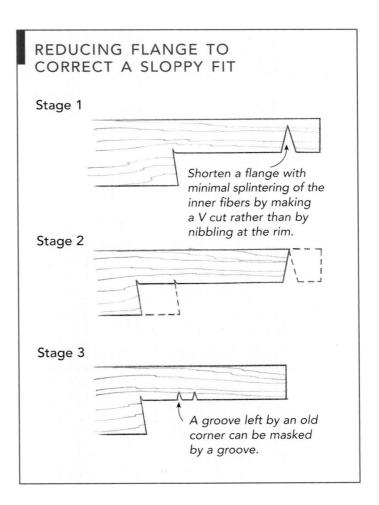

Stage 1

Shorten a flange with minimal splintering of the inner fibers by making a V cut rather than by nibbling at the rim.

Stage 2

Stage 3

A groove left by an old corner can be masked by a groove.

on p. 76). And if you do manage to jam the lid on, the slightest pressure against the axis from a cut or sanding will pull it straight off. If you use the tail center, you can't work all the end grain. The only solution is to re-turn the lid flange (as in steps 3 and 4 on p. 57), and that often makes the lid too big for the base. You then need to work back into the base as in the drawing on p. 77 or start again. Often it is best to start again with your errors well in mind rather than to contend with drastically altered proportions arising from the remainders of your original blank.

Screw-On Lids

In late Victorian times, huge numbers of wooden cases and boxes with screw-on lids were made to contain bottles and pills. (There is a large collection of these in the Pinto Collection of Treen in the Birmingham City Museum, England: a must-see for anyone interested in turnery or even small wooden artifacts in general.) In those days, threads were chased by hand, but today only a few turners, like Englishmen Bill Jones and Allan Batty, continue the tradition. It all looks so easy when you watch masters chasing threads by hand, but most people,

like myself, have opted for using a threading jig (see the photo below), which is much easier to learn.

A major attraction of screw-on lids is that they make turning a box profile a lot easier since they don't come off at the slightest hint of a catch. The steps for making a box with a screw-on lid are similar to those for a box with a suction-fit lid (see chapter 4). The inside of the lid is completed first, then fitted to the base after the inside is hollowed. Then the outside is finished.

The threads are cut on a jig that winds the flange past a cutter rotating at about 3,000 rpm to 5,000 rpm. The precise depth of the thread is determined by the number of threads per inch, or tpi, and the depth of cut is determined by adjusting the calibration wheel on the front of the jig. The threads per inch are dictated by the lead screw, which advances the work on the jig. For my Klein Design threading jig, I have lead screws to cut 10 tpi, 16 tpi, and 20 tpi.

To prepare the lid for threading, ensure that the flange is cylindrical and the sides straight. Turn a small recess with a chamfered inner lip (see the drawing on the facing page). The chamfer keeps the start of the thread from getting too thin and fragile.

A Klein Design threading jig. The chuck is transferred from the lathe to the spindle for the threads to be cut.

*A major attraction of screw-on lids is that they
make turning a box profile a lot easier.*

Cocobolo (left) and
kingwood boxes
with screw-on lids.

SCREW-ON LIDS

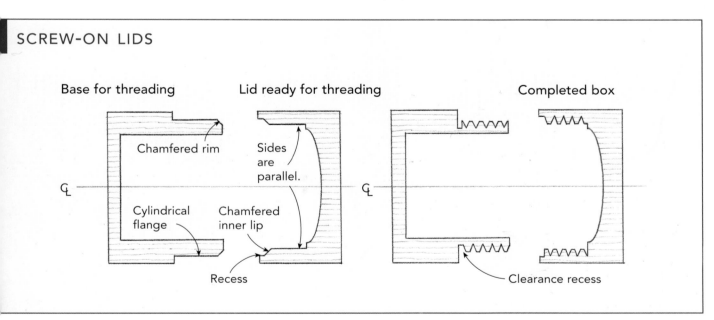

Base for threading

Chamfered rim

C̵L

Cylindrical
flange

Lid ready for threading

Sides
are
parallel.

Chamfered
inner lip

Recess

Completed box

C̵L

Clearance recess

MAKING A SCREW-ON LID

1 Once the lid flange has been prepared, unscrew the chuck with the lid in place and transfer it to the jig. Adjust the jig to bring the inner lip of the lid just within the diameter of the cutter. Here the cutting depth for 16 tpi is about ⁵⁄₆₄ in. (1.5mm).

2 Cut the thread. Three to five turns should give you a more-than-sufficient length of thread, but a couple more turns provide plenty of margin for error later as you line up the grain. The first thread of a pair is best cut in one pass. You will get a bit of microchipping on top of the thread, but this can be lightly sanded to leave a flat top. On softer woods it can help to flow thin cyanoacrylate adhesive over the flange to harden it before you cut the thread.

3 Finish the inside of the lid. I tend to wind the thread into the foot of the shoulder, so it usually needs re-turning. Lightly sand the top of the threads and polish the inside.

4 To establish the diameter of the base flange, measure the internal diameter of the lid and add some extra width from which to cut the thread. I allow ⅛ in. (3mm) for 16 tpi.

5 Turn the base flange to the diameter just established. Err on the side of caution and make the flange oversize rather than under. You can always cut the thread deeper, but you cannot reclaim it once it has gone. The length of the flange needs to be a minimum of three threads in length. Do not forget to chamfer the inner lip for the start of the thread.

6 Set the cutting depth in three steps. First, adjust the flange surface to the tip of the cutter. Second, back the flange rim clear of the cutter, then finally use the calibration knob to set the depth of cut.

7 Cut the base-flange thread. The problem here is that both cutter and flange are rotating in the same direction. The force of the cutter can unwind the chuck from the jig, so you should have a set screw to keep it in position. I do not have a screw, and therefore I need to keep a restraining hand on the chuck as the threading proceeds, which keeps my hand clear of the cutter too.

8 After cutting the thread, wind the base clear and test the lid fit. If too tight, take another light cut.

MAKING A SCREW-ON LID *(continued)*

9 Cut a recess for clearance at the end of the thread to ensure the lid will screw right up to the base shoulder easily. The narrow scraper used here was ground on the tang of an old skew chisel.

10 After lightly sanding the thread, put the lid on loosely, align the grain, and mark it. If the wood has particularly strong grain lines, there's no need to mark it.

11 Screw the lid up to the shoulder to assess the grain alignment.

12 Use the bevel side of a scraper to reduce the shoulder until the grain matches or your marks line up.

13 Here I have overcut the shoulder, but the grain is uniform enough that this is not a problem.

When there is a strong grain pattern, having the grain come into alignment as the lid screws tight enhances the quality of the box. African blackwood box, 2 in. (50mm) in diameter

Detail at the join disguises any shrinkage and swelling in the wood, which occurs with changing humidity.

The Join

The lid and base will inevitably move in relation to one another with changes in humidity and age. Time deforms everything and everybody, as we all know from personal experience. Boxes with no detailing at the join can look fine as they are completed and feel fine, too—for half an hour or so. However, with the slightest shrinkage or warping, you can feel the join and always a sharp shoulder.

It's not very nice. But if you create some detail at the join (see the photos on this page) any slight distortion in the wood is masked.

Detail, in the form of grooves or beads, can also help mask breaks in the grain pattern. Because of the way turned boxes are made, you are bound to be missing grain at least the length of the base flange. Even with very straight grain, exact matches are not that easy. Typical are the bocote boxes (see the photo above), where the match is good on the main verticals and so

The larger box joins in the center of the four beads, the smaller box beneath the beads. Bocote; c. 1990; 3 in. (75mm) in diameter.

It doesn't matter if the beads are on the base or lid—the visual impact will be the same.

WAYS TO DETAIL THE JOIN

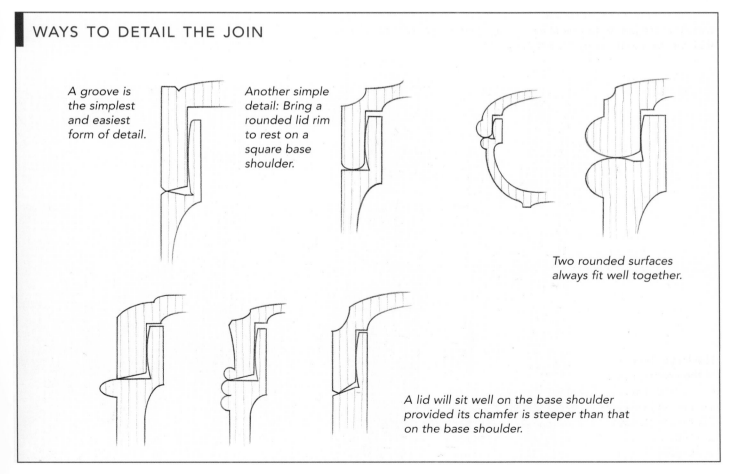

A groove is the simplest and easiest form of detail.

Another simple detail: Bring a rounded lid rim to rest on a square base shoulder.

Two rounded surfaces always fit well together.

A lid will sit well on the base shoulder provided its chamfer is steeper than that on the base shoulder.

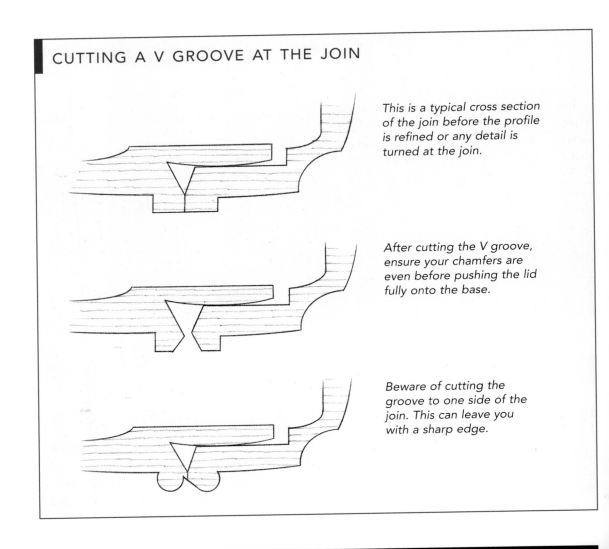

CUTTING A V GROOVE AT THE JOIN

This is a typical cross section of the join before the profile is refined or any detail is turned at the join.

After cutting the V groove, ensure your chamfers are even before pushing the lid fully onto the base.

Beware of cutting the groove to one side of the join. This can leave you with a sharp edge.

A shoulder inside the lid separates the end grain from the flanges, defining the two surfaces, which vary in smoothness.

striking that you tend not to notice that elsewhere other bits don't meet. Even though the grain doesn't match exactly, you need to look closely to see where the join is.

In addition to adding some detail you need to pay close attention to the exact shape of your rims and shoulders. The point to remember is that either the lid rim, the base shoulder, or both should be chamfered inward so that the two parts come together on a narrow edge (see the drawing on p. 85).

You will be detailing the join once the inside is finished. Assuming you have chamfered either the lid rim or the base shoulder as suggested, when you cut into the join you will create a space (see the drawing on the facing page). Chamfer the rims before you push the lid fully on. You will find it easier to cut equal chamfers and won't have one chamfer intruding on the other if you work to one side of the join.

Inside the Lid

I consider the inside of the lid as having three distinct areas and surfaces: the flange, which will fit over the base, the end grain, and the shoulder between.

The flanges should be sanded as little as possible in order to retain the turned diameter. When you sand, softer areas of grain are removed faster than harder areas, so the diameter will begin to vary, which affects the quality of the fit. If both lid and base flanges become slightly oval, the lid will slop over the base then twist to jam on. In the years when many of my boxes had this locking system, I found that people were impressed. But the grain never lines up in the jammed position so, knowing these were substandard fits, I learned to cut the flanges cleanly. Then all they need is a dab of 240 grit to remove ultrasharp corners on the rim.

The end grain is a different story. Here nothing is affected if it's a bit out of true. On some

Burl Boxes

This is about as large as a suction-fit lid needs to be. Few people have hands large enough to grasp larger diameters.

MATERIAL:	Eucalyptus burl
SIZES:	4⅛ in. by 5½ in. (105mm by 140mm) and 5⅛ in. by 5⅜ in. (130mm by 135mm)

Inside a lid, a shoulder between the flange and end grain serves as a barrier between the two.

Gidgee Boxes

If you mess up when cutting beads you can use a groove instead for much the same visual effect.

MATERIAL: Gidgee
SIZE: 1¾ in. by 4 in.

woods you might need to sand hard to get a good surface. I tend to leave a decorative feature. This not only adds strength to the lid, especially if there is a knob or finial, but also is easier to turn than some smooth dome or flat surface, and it's more interesting. But better yet for me as a production turner is that boxes with such detail sell for more than those without, so I score on all points.

A shoulder between the flange and end grain (see the top drawing on the facing page) serves as a barrier between the two—a line of demarcation that tells your eye to tell your brain to prepare your fingers for a possible difference in surface texture. The shoulder need not be very big. If you have a lid similar to the top left drawing on the facing page, you have a problem arising from sanding if you are trying not to touch the flange. As sanding proceeds, you lose the smooth transition from the cylindrical flange into the dome and there is a fuzzy change of texture that sends messages that the maker is not in control of the process. This might well be true, but there's no need to advertise it. In this situation a groove or two in the transition provides a boundary, or you could create a corner.

For these internal curves, use as big a scraper as possible, but only a small part of the edge at one time (see the bottom drawing on the facing page). By starting with the tool tilted up at the rim or down at center, you can raise or lower the handle to bring the edge through an arc as it cuts. This gives you greater precision than if you merely move the tool across the rest.

TRANSITION OPTIONS BETWEEN THE FLANGE AND END GRAIN

No transition

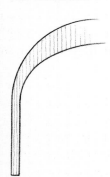

No transition between the flange and end grain can mean distortion during sanding.

Square transition

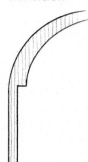

A square shoulder separates the flange and the end grain, giving more control during sanding.

Curved transition

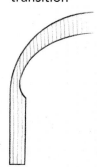

A curved transition also separates the flange and end grain but can leave the lid wall too thin.

CUTTING INTERNAL CURVES

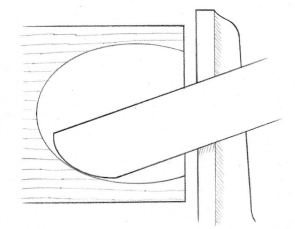

Use a larger rather than smaller scraper when cutting internal curves, even though you use the same amount of edge on each tool. If you use a scraper with a curve just tighter than the curve you want, you will find cutting a smooth curve much easier.

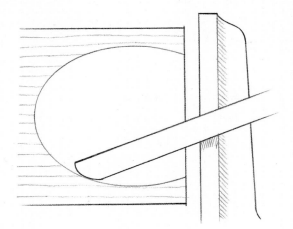

It is more difficult to cut a broad curve with a narrow tool.

6 DEEP HOLLOWING

Tall boxes challenge your technical skills, but they are worth the trauma when they're completed. (Box front right by Bob Krause.)

For a number of years I've made sets of spillikans, or pick-up sticks. People tend to be bowled over by the slenderness of the sticks, but the sticks merely take time to turn; the box is the difficult bit, requiring a lot of skill if you are to make a really good job of it. I like to turn and decorate the end grain both inside and out, and to do that kind of deep hollowing and delicate work, it's necessary to learn how to control the leverage or to find a way around the problem. On the end grain of long and narrow forms, even turning simple grooves can be tricky, while finials or more complicated details are woefully difficult. In the end, though, the end result is worth the trauma and general expending of nervous energy.

All the really nasty problems that occur when hollowing deep into end grain involve leverage. As you work farther into the end grain, the point of cut becomes ever more distant from the rest, and the task of controlling the tool becomes increasingly difficult. The simple answer to deep hollowing would appear to be to bore out the waste using a drill mounted in the tailstock. But you might not want a cylindrical shaft in your box base, let alone the hole made by the center spur. Or your budget might not be high enough to accommodate the cost of a drill or boring tool capable of drilling larger holes.

When I made my first spillikan box about 25 years ago, I considered boring both base and lid, but the two drills required would have cost almost as much as what I assumed to be a one-time job was worth; also the tail center I had then was off-center, so I couldn't bore anything on the lathe anyway. I did the boring by hand, using a square-end scraper, and I did it again and again and again for the next 90 or so spillikan boxes. Then I realized that my spillikan sets were a sort of slow production line and that I could justify the purchase of a couple of drills, and I have used these ever since. However, there are plenty of other situations where things have to be done by hand, and, when accuracy isn't so important, I find it faster, as well as more enjoyable, to apply the skill. Much of my deep-hollowing practice has come through making pencil pots as a production item, where the wide opening provides plenty of margin for error.

Boring End Grain by Hand

Boring into end grain by hand can be hard work if the wood is particularly tough. The idea is to remove the core, then hollow the box in a series of steps using a long and strong scraper with a handle at least 20 in. (500mm) long (see the drawing on p. 92). The trick, as with all turning, is to not push the tool too forcefully into the wood and to use only a portion of the edge at one time. Expend your energy into controlling the leverage, not forcing the tool into the wood. Run the lathe at a lower speed, around 1,000 rpm or less. The lower the speed, the less dramatic the catch when things go wrong, and you can be sure that one day they will.

All the really nasty problems that occur when hollowing deep into end grain involve leverage.

Use the long point of a skew chisel to make a small V pilot hole for the drill at the center of the blank.

The core is removed with a depth drill to within ⅛ in. (3mm) of the required depth.

The trick, as with all turning, is to not push the tool too forcefully into the wood and to use only a portion of the edge at one time.

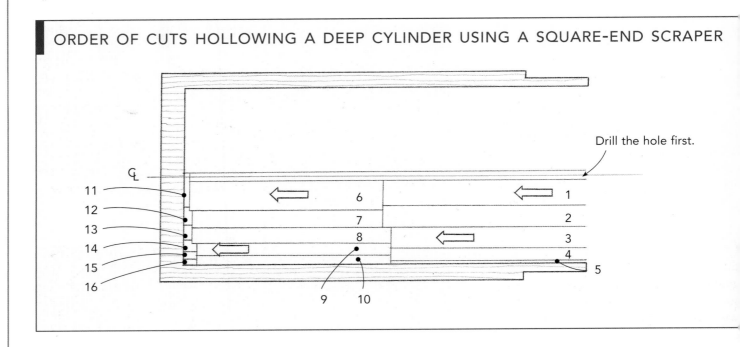

ORDER OF CUTS HOLLOWING A DEEP CYLINDER USING A SQUARE-END SCRAPER

Drill the hole first.

Spillikan box ends; 1978; putumuju.

Having trued the blank, make a small V at the center with the long point of a skew chisel, keeping the chisel flat on the rest (see the top photo on p. 91). Use a depth drill to remove the core to within ⅛ in. (3mm) of your required depth (see the bottom photo on p. 91). (I measure this again more carefully at the end of cut 6.)

Using tape, I mark the depth I need to hollow on the blade of a heavy scraper (see the top photo on the facing page). For a 3¾-in.- (95mm) diameter base, I use a 1-in. (25mm) scraper with the left corner ground to about 88° (see the drawing on the facing page). The rest is set at center height and the tool is kept horizontal. The edge will cut at a point the thickness of the tool above center.

For the initial cuts (2 to 4), you can use about half the edge to take a reasonable shaving.

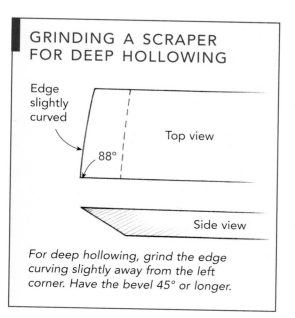

GRINDING A SCRAPER FOR DEEP HOLLOWING

Edge slightly curved

88°

Top view

Side view

For deep hollowing, grind the edge curving slightly away from the left corner. Have the bevel 45° or longer.

I use a heavy scraper to hollow out the blank. The tape on the scraper serves as a depth gauge.

I never try to go the whole depth in one pass during the initial cuts. Typically the wood starts grabbing at the edge after about 2 in. (50mm), so I go as far as is comfortable for cut 1, then widen the hole to about the same depth with cuts 2 to 4. This allows me to get the feel of the particular piece of wood before controlling the leverage becomes increasingly difficult during the remainder of the cuts. Check that the opening is cylindrical after 1 in. (25mm) of cut 4 has been made.

Note how the width of the shaving narrows as the cuts move away from the center (see the bottom photo at right). You need to take a smaller cut because of the leverage exerted against the point where the chuck grabs the blank, particularly when starting the cut at the rim. Cuts 1 and 6 are just off-center and well within the diameter of the chuck jaws, so any pressure is directly against the chuck. You are most likely to pull the wood from the chuck at the start of cuts 4 and 5. You can get a hint of the forces involved by grasping a cylinder in your fingertips and applying pressure to different parts of the end grain (see the photo on p. 94). As you press against the rim you can feel

As the cut moves away from the center, the width of the shaving narrows.

the cylinder pivoting against your thumb, whereas pressure at the center is evenly distributed. You can experiment using everyday objects like a 35mm film container or similar plastic container.

As the cut proceeds, it is relatively easy to cope with the leverage because it increases evenly as you cut farther from the rest. Align the scraper

Tulipwood Boxes

Very bright when first turned, sadly this wood soon mellows on the outside where it's exposed to light. Tall forms are emphasized by pronounced grain situations.

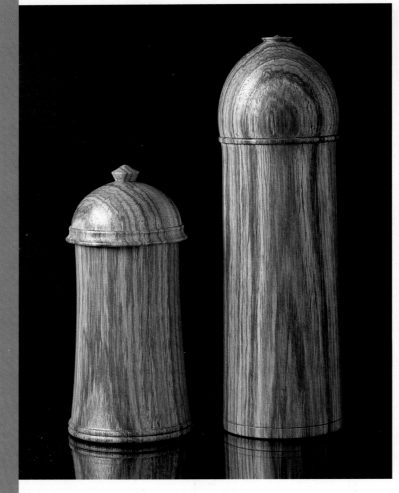

MATERIAL: Tulipwood
SIZES: 1¾ in. by 4⁵⁄₁₆ in.
and 6¼ in.
(45mm by 110mm
and 160mm)

Here's a quick way to get a feel for the forces involved when hollowing. Grip the cylinder with your fingertips and press the end grain in different locations.

handle under your forearm, with your elbow over the end of the handle to transfer any catches up into your shoulder (see the top photo on the facing page). Your right hand should be on the ferrule by the time you get to cut 5.

Keeping the tool horizontal is difficult because the pressure of the wood tends to push the tool's edge down. If the edge is tilted down, the hole you turn will narrow from the rim because the lower left side of the tool blade will rub the wood and the tilting eases the tool toward center.

If you raise the edge above horizontal, the hole will widen from the rim, and most likely the tool will catch. You can cope with such an event during the initial cuts when you want to get the guts out as quickly as possible and can rechuck the blank. When the wall becomes thinner, a catch usually splits the job beyond repair.

You can use the side of the scraper as a jig to help keep the tool horizontal, provided you make the first 1 in. (25mm) of the hollow cylindrical. Having established the cylinder, all you need to do is ensure that the top left side of the

To counteract snatches and catches, position the handle of the scraper under your forearm with your elbow over the end of the handle.

As you cut nearer the bottom, the sound of the cut changes, indicating that you are nearing the solid end grain.

Check that your initial opening is cylindrical, then use that surface to jig the tool. Keep the upper left side of the tool blade rubbing the wood to maintain the cylinder shape all the way to the bottom.

tool blade maintains contact with the cylindrical surface (see the top right photo on the facing page). With practice you will be able to feel this rather than having to bend over to see what's happening. I stop the lathe and use calipers to check that the sides are parallel at cut 4 (or even 5) if I'm feeling confident. When you are new to the concept, though, measure sooner and concentrate on keeping the hollow cylindrical from the first cut.

As you cut nearer the bottom, the sound of the cut changes, indicating that you are nearing the solid end grain. Cuts 6 to 9 each stop just short of the previous cut to prevent the whole of the edge from suddenly contacting the end grain. This is a big danger area, where the leverage is at the maximum. If you suddenly have the pressure on the cutting edge doubled or tripled as it hits end grain, you'll need the strength of Samson to control the catch. If the form is long and thin and there is not much space for the tool to operate, the wood usually explodes, and you must start again.

Cuts 11 to 16, which clean up the base, are the most difficult, chiefly because you cannot

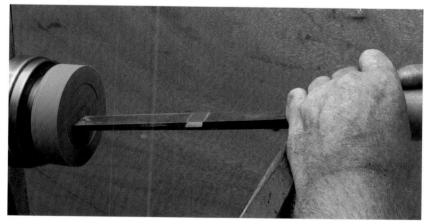

Practice turning the end grain inside deep boxes on a waste block with the rest set back so you can see what is happening. Here the cut is 8 in. (200mm) over the rest.

TIPS FOR TURNING THE PROFILE AND END GRAIN

If you tried the exercise of testing leverage by holding the cylinder and pressing on the end grain, then you realize that turning the end grain demands a delicate touch if you are going to avoid catches and keep the work on the lathe. It is difficult to grip either the lid or the base with absolute security, but there are a few tricks that in some situations might give you moral support, although not much else.

For a start, aim to use the full length of each blank, rather than parting off and reverse-chucking in order to turn the top of the lid or the bottom of the base. By using the full length, you get the most difficult turning done while there is the least risk. So true the blank and turn the top of the lid and the bottom of the base before rechucking each part for hollowing. Frequently I will include a rim detail that fits the chuck, as on the foot of the box in the photo at right. Working this way, the ends will be true and look fine, although the bits between might not stand intense scrutiny.

The crucial visual bits on any box are the join and the rims at either end; having them look right is half the battle. If you have end-grain detail slightly off-center, sand the edges round and fudge the rim. Areas between the join and the rim that are slightly eccentric can be sanded to meld together. It takes a keen eye to see what is actually happening.

Laburnum spillikans container; 1979; 9⅜ in. by 1⅞ in. (240mm by 48mm). The groove at the foot is part decorative, but mostly practical. The foot and base were turned to fit the chuck before being hollowed, providing a secure grip for the blank as work proceeded.

CUSTOM TAIL-CENTER SUPPORT

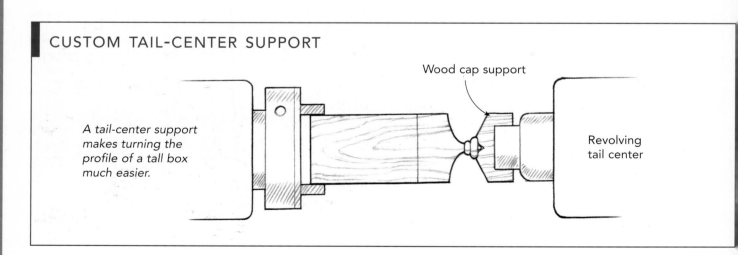

A tail-center support makes turning the profile of a tall box much easier.

Wood cap support

Revolving tail center

When completing the profile on a long box, the slightest excessive tool pressure, especially against the axis, can pull the lid off. Catches are often serious, needing cyanoacrylate glue to repair the odd split. One solution is to tape the lid on at the tight-fit stage for added security as you do the end of the lid (see the top photo at right), but this does not help when you come to detail the join.

A better method is to use a flat tail-center support or one turned to fit the lid detail (see the drawing on the facing page and the center and bottom photos at right). There should be minimal pressure against the lid from the tail center—simply wind it in to rest against the wood.

To turn a cylinder, establish your diameters by pulling (rather than pushing) the calipers over the profile in several places. Then, unless the grain is absolutely straight, use the peeling cut to true a cylindrical form.

Detailing the top of this 10¾-in. (275mm) box was going to be tricky because of its size, so I taped the lid at the join in addition to providing the usual hand support.

If your tail center does not offer a range of spurs or shaped supports, it is easy to turn one that fits as a cap over most revolving centers.

A custom-made tail-center support ensures the lid stays on without damaging the end grain while the profile is completed. Here I use a peeling cut, keeping the skew chisel flat on the rest.

HOLLOWING A DEEP ROUNDED FORM

When the internal form is rounded it is often faster to remove the inside using a gouge for cuts 1-7, then a square-end scraper for cuts 8-12, before completing the job using a round-nose scraper (cuts 13 and 14).

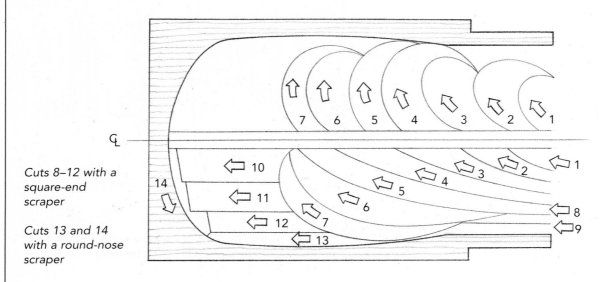

Cuts 1–7:
back-hollowing
with gouge

Drill the center
hole first.

Cuts 1–7:
hollowing with
a gouge into
the end grain

Cuts 8–12 with a
square-end
scraper

Cuts 13 and 14
with a round-nose
scraper

see what is happening. Even if you can get light in there—and there is a fiber-optic widget for tool junkies for just this situation—chances are there will be too many shavings in the way.

You have to feel what is happening when working at the bottom of a tight space, so it pays to practice on a bit of end grain with the rest set well back so you can see while you get a feel for the cut (see the bottom photo on p. 95).

For cut 11 at center, start with the tool pitched down and just below center, then ease your weight on the end of the handle to bring the edge up to start cutting. You will feel a slight bounce on the end of the tool as the edge contacts the wood. Firm up your grip and bring the edge through center to cut the fibers cleanly. The pale dust just in from the right corner of the scraper indicates where the point of the cut is. The slightly curved edge of the

scraper means that on either side of this point, the edge is clear of the wood. The right corner of the scraper will be the far side of center but not on the wood.

Next, ease the left corner of the tool slowly and steadily away from center. Again, this is when you need to have the edge slightly curved. Use only ⅛ in. (3mm) or so from the left corner; the remainder curves clear of the end grain.

Another way to make the inside cuts is to use the back-hollowing technique shown in the drawing above.

In an effort to show how clever I could be, I took to decorating the two internal end-grain surfaces of my deeper boxes, usually with a couple of grooves, just to show that the inside was turned, not drilled. To make beads, I used narrow skewed scrapers, using much the same technique as when turning flat end grain, but going even more gently. With this method catches are usually terminal for the box, so being gentle is very important. Eventually a mishap led me to a far easier way of achieving a better result.

Drilling End Grain

When I started drilling out my spillikan boxes, it was my practice to clean up the bottom as just described. But one day I mismeasured and drilled through the base, leaving me with a tube. I had already made the lid and had no spare blanks in suitable wood, just a few off-cuts. Fortunately the wood was uniformly dark, so I turned up a nicely decorated little end-grain disk insert for the base. On the inside, the join couldn't be seen close up and was disguised as a corner. On the underside, a couple of grooves hid what glueline there was. The base fit tightly and was fixed with cyanoacrylate adhesive. I wish I'd thought of this years before.

As a result of this discovery, I now make deeper straight-sided boxes by drilling out a cylinder before inserting a lid or base made from a section lopped from each end of the blank. Thus a blank is divided in four or in three (see the drawing at right). If you make the lid shorter, getting at the end grain is not as difficult, so you can make the whole lid at once without an insert. Be sure to mark the parts so you can reassemble them in the same alignment.

To drill out either the lid or base, you will need an accurate tail center (see the centers on p. 6 for how to check accuracy). Use a key chuck to hold the drill and just wind the drill into the blank (see the photo above). If the depth you want to drill is more than the travel of the tail-center quill, stop the lathe, back off the drill, move the tail center in, then carry on. On the drill, mark the farthest depth you can go if you don't want to go through the bottom. I use little bits of tape for my markers.

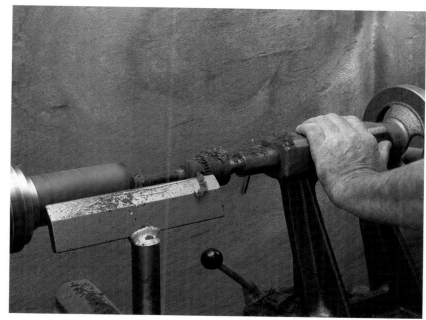

A quick way to remove the center of a blank is to use a drill mounted in the tail center. Make sure to mark the depth on the bit.

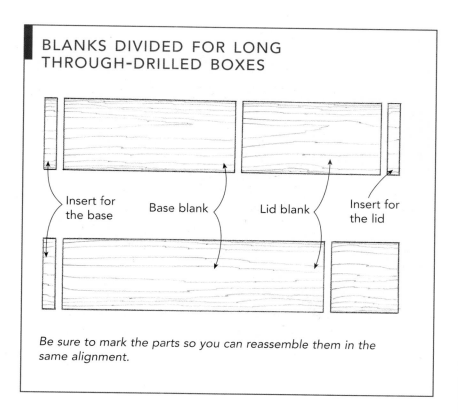

BLANKS DIVIDED FOR LONG THROUGH-DRILLED BOXES

Insert for the base

Base blank

Lid blank

Insert for the lid

Be sure to mark the parts so you can reassemble them in the same alignment.

MAKING AND FITTING AN INSERT

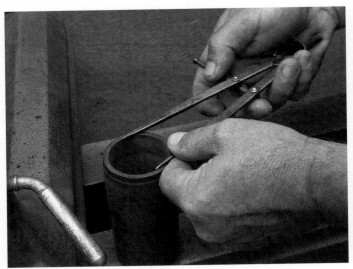

1 Use calipers to measure the diameter of the cylinder, then turn a taper that thickens from the rim.

2 Hold the cylinder over the taper to obtain a burnish mark that establishes the desired diameter. The nearer this mark is to the end, the better, because the rim of the insert needs to fit tightly against the cylinder when in place. Turn away any part of the flange to the right of the burnished line.

3 Having established a tight fit, turn the end grain. Ensure that the underside of a base insert is recessed so that when it is fitted there is no question of the bottom being other than concave.

4 Cut a small groove on the diameter of the insert in which to locate the chuck jaws so you can turn the other face accurately.

INSERTS

Do not sand the cylinder before fitting the insert because this will distort the diameter and make a near-invisible fit difficult.

Inserts for bases

Note that the underside is recessed so that the base will sit flat.

Inserts for lids

I like some finial or decorative top for the lid.

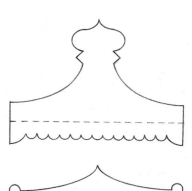

5 Ensure the grain is correctly aligned, then push the insert into position and check that it sits square before running thin cyanoacrylate adhesive into the join.

If your fingers cannot reach the bottom of a hollow,
you will need a sanding stick.

Sanding the Inside of a Deep Hollow

If your fingers cannot reach the bottom of a hollow, you will need a sanding stick. For the inside of small-diameter boxes where my fingers won't fit, I have short lengths of dowel variously shaped on a sander to match either curved or cylindrical spaces. For larger jobs where my fingers are too short to reach, I have a heavier dowel with a saw cut down the center by which to secure the abrasive sheets (see the photos on the facing page).

Coarse-grained timbers are likely to suffer some tearout as hollowing proceeds. Often you can have situations where there is not enough wood to risk another cut or where the wood just will not cut cleanly. Inside a base, where the surface does not have to fit anything and concentricity is not an issue, I have no qualms about getting in with 60-grit abrasive. Mostly I use old sanding disks, which have a good life long after they cease to be effective for power sanding bowls. Although sanding is an inefficient way of cutting (in relation to a scraping), coarse abrasives can remove a lot of material. If the flange rim becomes eccentric, round it over to disguise the fact.

A deft touch is required for sanding lids because you don't want to touch the flange and distort it. The solution is to do the coarse sanding, then turn the flange before working through the finer grades of abrasive.

To polish deep insides, wrap a rag around the same stick that the abrasive was on (see the photo below).

In the final analysis, deeper boxes can either be drilled out, which is somewhat monotonous and a small challenge to the adventurous spirit, or hand-turned, which is an increasing physical challenge the deeper you go. And as you work farther and farther over the rest, the nervous strain increases. These are not objects I hurry to make for pleasure: On the one hand I can barely stand the nervous strain, whereas on the other, if I drill, I miss the challenge. Somewhere between these extremes are projects that stretch the skills and offer scope for embellishment and fulfillment. But before I consider these, let's take a look in the next chapter at some of the ways we can alter a box with surface or applied decoration.

Wrap a rag around a dowel to polish deep insides.

SANDING HARD-TO-REACH DEEP HOLLOWS

This quick-to-make "tool" is a real help in getting into the recess in a deep vessel. Bandsaw a kerf down the center of a dowel and about the length of a quarter sheet of sandpaper. Choose a dowel of sufficient diameter to provide strength and allow easy bandsawing.

1 Insert the abrasive sheet into the dowel that's been cut down the center.

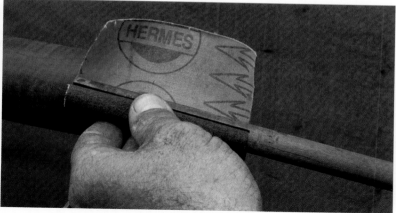

2 Wrap the abrasive sheet around the dowel.

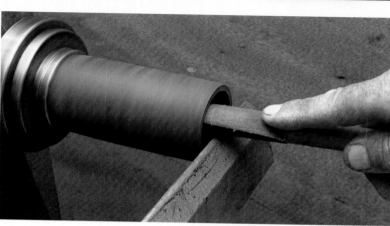

3 Insert the abrasive-wrapped end of the dowel into the deep hollow to sand the inside.

CHAPTER

7 SURFACE DECORATION

Small wooden objects like boxes are not ideal vehicles to display the best grain a tree has to offer. In part, this is because the swirling mass of broad patterns so admired on furniture, doors and floors, and turned bowls are side-grain patterns, not end-grain patterns. Logs with strong medullary rays can be quartersawn to yield wonderful figures, but on a cylinder, especially a small one like a box, you get only a couple of glimpses of this, and on the end grain you get only strong lines.

On the laburnum box at left in the top photo on the facing page, you can see how the growth-ring lines make the strong end-grain pattern flow down to the profile, remaining tight in two areas and broadening to the eyelike pattern between. The casuarina box on the right in the same photo has strong medullary rays, which, when sliced lengthwise, yield the loop-and-ribbon figure, but still this only hints at the broader patterns. For good figure or flashy grain on a tightly curved box profile, fiddleback or bird's-eye grain is a better bet.

Turning on a small scale generally demands tight grain for ease of working, and although a few woods like ash disprove the rule (see the left box in the bottom photo on the facing page), boxes are rarely remarkable for their grain. Detail, texture, or color is often needed to make stark forms more appealing to those of us who can't cope with outright simplicity. For ornamentation, turners rarely look further than beads and grooves, but there are a number of other techniques that can change the surface or affect how we perceive the whole.

Since wood was first spun on a lathe,
beads, grooves, and coves have been the turner's
favored means of decorating.

On the laburnum box (left), the growth-ring lines make a strong end-grain pattern. On the casuarina box (right), the medullary rays create a nice loop-and-ribbon figure.

Most commercial hardwoods need some decoration because while they're rich in color, they're also close grained, like the padauk (second from left and far right). Ash (left) is one of the few open-grained hardwoods that works well on a small scale, with a grain strong enough to carry the piece visually. The casuarina (rear) is bright salmon-red when first cut and very eye-catching, but it soon mellows.

Beads across the top of a lid work especially well for woods that have no strong features. Imbuya; 3 in. (75mm) in diameter.

Turned Decoration

Since wood was first spun on a lathe, beads, grooves, and coves have been the turner's favored means of decorating. Why bother carving a surface when, with the roll of your wrist, you can create a nice little bead or cove? On boxes, beads have traditionally been used around the join and to emphasize the lid or foot, as well as to create frivolous finials or frame inlays. And they are useful for softening angles and corners.

Beads or grooves are commonly used to detail and obscure the join. A single bead on the rim of a lid makes a good frame for a slightly convex top, defining the end grain like a picture. You can also use beads where the line of the profile changes direction, especially if there is a join (see the photo below). I like to use beads across the top of a lid (see the photo at left), particularly if the wood has no strong features. A little cone at the center looks better and is easier to make than a plain dome. And

A good place to use beads is where the line of profile changes direction, as in these boxes of casuarina, about 3 in. (75mm) in diameter.

The big, bold beads define the character of this box. Casuarina; 5 in. (125mm) in diameter. (Box by Guillio Marcolongo.)

This box has a spontaneity about it. Note the subtle curve of the profile and how the beads narrow the farther they are from the join. Casuarina; 2 in. (50mm) in diameter. (Box by Guillio Marcolongo.)

If the join line looks isolated from other lid details, use grooves to adjust the proportions.

This is a very successful box made from very unpromising aspen, a notoriously soft timber. Every portion except the base has chatter-work decoration, which is further enhanced with color and a cabachon on top. Aspen; 2 in. (50mm) in diameter. (Box by A. Hampe.)

Turban box. (Box by Steven Gray.)

sometimes a lid requires a band of decoration to balance the form.

Beads are more difficult to turn than grooves, but if you mess them up, don't worry— more often than not you can use some grooves in their place to create much the same visual impact (see the top photos and the bottom left photo on p. 107). Grooves are the simplest and quickest decoration a turner can apply, but they should be cut rather than scraped to look their best and be small rather than huge. When the lid is deep, the join line can look odd stuck on its own away from supporting detail, so use grooves as a simple way of balancing a form (see the bottom right photo on p. 107).

Chatter Work

My turning education instilled in me the belief
that chatter marks are a sign of extreme inepti-
tude to be eliminated. But later I discovered
there is a long tradition of using this technique
in pottery, and in the early 20th century there
was a company in Japan turning a range of treen
in ebony using chatter work for surface decoration. I flirted with the technique on bowls in
the late 1970s, but it was American Dennis
Stewart who popularized the use of chatter
work on woodturnings in the late '80s.

Chatter work, as the name implies, is a technique where the tool is made to vibrate in order
to create a regular pattern on the wood. No pattern can ever be repeated, so it is a good way of
making each piece unique. I have created some
good patterns using a short length of thick
bandsaw blade with the teeth ground off, but
Stewart has designed a tool for the job that is
difficult to beat (see the photo at right). It
works particularly well on hard end grain such
as African blackwood and the acacias.

Chatter work can be created using a Stewart System chatter tool.

Off-center patterns can be made using an eccentric chuck mounted in a conventional chuck. African blackwood; 2⅜ in. (60mm) in diameter.

The fluting on this lid is typical of ornamental turning, a whole craft unto itself. Kingwood; 2⅛ in. (55mm) in diameter. (Maker unknown; English, c. 1986.)

Off-Center Patterns

Ornamental or complex turning involves creating all manner of fluting or off-center patterns on a preturned surface (see the photo at left). It is a whole craft unto itself developed in the mid-18th century when John Jacob Holtzapffel became the name synonymous with ornamental lathes and turning. His complex machines were able to create a seemingly infinite number of patterns and are still much sought after and hugely expensive. Less expensive are modern lathes designed for similar work, but you still need to be seriously interested to make the investment. What I offer here is a very inexpensive way of achieving off-center patterns similar to that used by Hans Weissflog. All you need is a delicate touch and patience. But be warned: What you might think of as a delicate touch might not be half delicate enough.

Patterns like the ones in the photo above can be turned using an off-center jam chuck turned into a rectangular blank gripped by two jaws of

This is a fine example of the restrained use of mixed mediums—the ebony line on the lid rim adds interest to the profile while visually balancing the inlay. Alternative ivory, ebony, polymer clay; 1¾ in. (45mm) in diameter. (Box by Kip Christensen; inlay by Sherri Haab. Photo by Dan Haab.)

the four-jaw self-centering chuck. So you have one chuck within another. The concept is simple: Once the lid is mostly finished, with the inside completed and the top trued, it is mounted on an off-center chuck. By rotating the lid on the off-center chuck, you relocate the center of the pattern to a different part of the lid. To regularize the pattern, the lid is divided with radial lines. Four centers are easiest to lay out, requiring two lines through the center at 90° to one another. Bisecting the angle between these lines will give you eight centers.

Inserts

Exceptional pieces of wood or other bits and pieces can be inlaid to contrast with the main material (see the photos above and at right). If you have a stub of attractive end grain left in the chuck after parting off some job, true it up and keep it. I have a box of disks that will make good inserts. The disks are cylindrical, with a flat face and straight, parallel sides, so they fit a

African blackwood with thornbush inlay; 3 in. (75mm) in diameter.

TURNING OFF-CENTER PATTERNS

In the photos here, I use a template to mark out three centers on the lid. A builder's offcut from a 3½-in. by 1⅜-in. (90mm by 35mm) pine wall stud provides a blank for the chuck, which is turned to fit the lid, then moved off-center.

3 Turn a jam chuck into which, or on which, the lid fits tightly. This lid is threaded, so it fits into a hole rather than over a spigot. Unthreaded lids are easier to chuck over a spigot, just like fitting a lid to a base.

1 I use a template to lay out the three radii for a trefoil pattern. Mark the radial lines down the side as well. The template is made from ³⁄₆₄-in. (1mm) plastic scavenged from a photographic-slides box, but any thin, stiff plastic will do.

2 In a chuck with two of the jaws removed, locate a short length of wood about 1 in. (25mm) off-center. Turn the lathe on in order to establish center, then mark a line through center along which you will align the radial lines on the lid.

4 Mount the lid on the chuck, ensuring that one of the radial lines is aligned with the centerline on the chuck. Move the wood chuck away from center until you have the center located where you want it on the lid. Check this by holding a pencil against the wood as you rotate the chuck by hand. In this instance I got it right on the third attempt. Tighten the chuck jaws and check the alignment in case tightening the jaws has pulled the top of the lid out of true. Note that the wood chuck is now better balanced within the jaws, reducing any possible vibration.

5 Turn the detail. Here I use a small skew chisel on its side as a scraper to turn the design because I can flip the tool over to get into the corners from either direction to form the bead. Any light sanding should be done now, since relocating the lid into this precise position later could be exceedingly difficult.

7 Finally, relocate the lid on the third radial line. A groove on the side of the lid is useful if you have to lever it from the chuck.

6 To repeat the design on the next radius, pry the lid off and relocate it so that one of the other radial lines is aligned with the centerline on the chuck.

8 Once the off-center work is completed, you can return the lid to its base and finish the box profile. I often turn any center detail at this stage, as you can see on the completed gidgee box, which is 2½ in. (65mm) in diameter.

Rippled white ash with black onyx cabachon inlay. Note the small bead that frames the cabachon. (Boxes by Ray Key.)

A turned ring of African blackwood was glued on the lid rim of this 2-in. (50mm) tulipwood box to compensate for the parting cut and overlap on the flange. (Box by Bonnie Klein.)

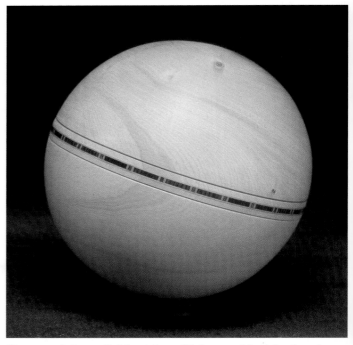

Commercially available strips of inlay are ideal for bands, like this one added to a spherical box made in 1993. (Box by Stephen Hughes. Photo by Ken Hatton.)

cylindrical recess exactly. Woodturning suppliers often keep a range of inserts (see the cabachons in the top photo on the facing page).

We tend to think of inlay being only in the lids, but it can be turned from solid wood or bought in strips to insert as a band (see the bottom photos on the facing page). A contrasting band snaps a form into life, and fine grooves on either side can subtly enhance the symmetry while disguising the join.

Texture

Woodworkers tend to go for ultrasmooth surfaces, but there are alternatives. A surface cleanly cut by a tool is not as glossy smooth as one that's sanded, but with handling it will develop a wonderful patina. Texture can also help hide defects in the wood or break up a surface to make it more interesting. Try playing around with textures. If you don't like what you get, you can always sand it smooth.

One of my all-time-favorite turned pieces is New Zealander Sören Berger's storage pot, which has been doing its job on his kitchen counter for about 25 years (see the photo at right on p. 116). The surface, which is off the tool, has never been sanded, oiled, or polished. Any abrasion and patina is from handling, and the piece is high on my list of turnings likely to be treasured for centuries. The grooves on the profile are actually one spiral left by the gouge as Berger made the final cut. Note the slightly concave sides and the way the top of the lid flares out to the rim. Abrasives would deaden a form as good as this, stealing its spontaneity.

I also like sand-blasted surfaces, but I rarely get near a powerful machine and certainly cannot justify buying one. An alternative is to use wire brushes to wear away the softer grain (see the top left photo on p. 116). A swirling texture is achieved by rotating a drill-mounted brass brush against the direction of the wood as it spins on the lathe. Concentric rings can

Citadel Series Boxes

These boxes have small containing spaces suited to single rings. The lids are loose-fit to be removed using one hand. Their whimsical shape suggests the towers of a fortress.

MATERIAL: Jarrah burl
SIZES: c. 4 in. (100mm) diameter

Try playing around with textures. If you don't like what you get, you can always sand it smooth.

A spinning brush held against the spinning wood removes softer grain and leaves swirling lines.

Storage pot, c. 1982. This is one of my favorite turned pieces. The surface grooves are actually one spiral left by the final pass of a gouge. English sycamore; 8 in. (200mm) in diameter. (Box by Sören Berger.)

The lid is mounted over the chuck jaws for texturing. This is a handy way to rechuck lids for re-turning or texturing. Here the flange fits over the jaw shoulders.

be created by holding a wire brush against the spinning wood; texture by easing the side into a bandsaw blade with the bandsaw table tilted about 45° to create the angled cut. The surface is then buffed by hand with a stiff brush, and oiled.

If you want to restrict the texture to either lid or base, expand the chuck jaws to grip the work from the inside so the lid is mounted over the chuck jaws (see the photo at left).

I sign my light-colored woods with a pyrographer's wood-burning pen and my dark or very hard woods with an engraving tool (see the top right and bottom photos on the facing page). But these tools can also be used to create grooves to give a box some texture (see the top left photo on the facing page).

Gidgee box. The textured lid was made using a pyrographer's wood-burning pen. (Lid design by Terry Baker.)

A pyrographer's wood-burning pen and an engraving tool (above) can both be used to add texture. However, these tools are used mostly for signing work (left).

Carving

Across the world there is a long tradition among generations of woodworkers of chiseling patterns into wood, but turners have rarely bothered, using the more rapidly produced beads, coves, and moldings at their disposal. Carving patterns may be time-consuming, but if you are not in production commercially, or aiming for a rarefied gallery market, so what. Enjoyable hours spent in the making yield years of delight.

More basic random carving around the lid can be done by easing the rim ⅟₃₂ in. (1mm) into the bandsaw blade. This is a very quick way of texturing near-vertical surfaces, and by using a wedge-shaped jig it is possible to put similar patterns on angled surfaces. Always ensure that there is support or solid wood directly under the point where the saw is cutting, otherwise the wood could be snatched into the blade taking your fingers with it. (See also the drawings on pp. 26 and 28.)

The carved facets on this box have developed a wonderful patina from years of handling. Rimu; 4⅜ in. (110mm) in diameter. (Box by Sören Berger. Photo by Paul McCormack.)

Plum Pudding Box; Tasmanian blackwood and huon pine; 2 in. (50mm) in diameter. (Box by Kath Bretag. Photo by Michal Kluvanek.)

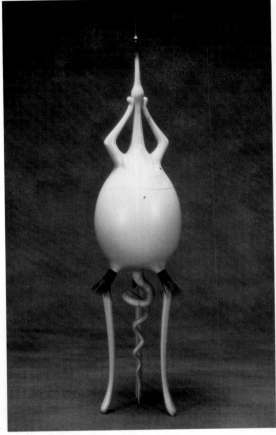

Evolving Egg VI, 1994. Made from a single piece of huon pine, the legs of this box were part-turned as a cylindrical form at the base of the egg, then cut off and carved before being reattached with threaded brass pins for strength. (Box by Stephen Hughes. Photo by Ken Hatton.)

Burning

By presenting a gas-torch flame at an angle you can burn just the corners of details, such as the rim pattern, highlighting the form. Then the surface should be sanded again with 240-grit or finer paper as desired. The boxes in the top photos on p. 136 were sanded to 240 grit, then scorched. Heavier sanding cuts that go through the scorching to the paler wood beneath give some wonderful cloudy effects that look even better once oiled.

The random carving around the lid of this box was done by scoring the edge on the bandsaw. Jarrah burl, carved and scorched; 4⅛ in. (105mm) in diameter.

Citadel Series Box

The outside was first sanded, then charred using a propane gas torch, then sanded again to create an ancient look. During the final sanding, gold paint was rubbed into the cracks to add a hint of sparkle.

MATERIAL:	Jarrah burl
SIZE:	8 in. by 9⅞ in. (200mm by 250mm)

8 VARIATIONS ON THE BASIC BOX

Once you become familiar with the standard box-making format, you'll probably want to try some variations. The boxes in this chapter are made following the basic steps set out in chapter 4, but each goes beyond the standard format. And so here you will find techniques and tips that will help you turn just about any type of box you want, from a box with a sculptured profile to a box that resembles Saturn to a box with a specific purpose, like a drill container.

The information is purposely general so that you can create boxes of your own, rather than replicate those shown here. As you work through the ideas in this chapter, let an overall impression of a piece pervade your subconscious, then allow your tool-handling and grinding idiosyncrasies to impinge on your turning so your own style develops, which it will unless it's rigorously checked.

Many of the boxes here are suited to production. If you intend selling boxes as part of your livelihood, you will need to streamline production as much as possible. Rule one is to concentrate on one wood at a time so you get to know it. If you dart from one species to another, it is difficult to pick up the nuances of the working characteristics of any particular wood, so do runs in one wood even if you want to make one-off pieces. By using one wood for several days at a time, you become very attuned to all its little quirks and spot potential problems well before they occur, saving hours of frustration and wasted time.

Don't copy directly. Let an overall impression of a piece pervade your subconscious, then allow your tool-handling and grinding idiosyncrasies to impinge on your turning so your own style develops.

I like to work in batches of six, getting into a rhythm by making all the lids, then fitting all the lids to their bases and completing the profiles before turning all the bottoms. It would be more efficient to work through bigger batches but also more tedious since you don't see finished pieces until later in the day, or even the week. I like seeing another six boxes completed every couple of hours.

Retaining the Bark

Some woods retain their bark, giving you the opportunity to keep it in the finished piece (see the photos below and at right). Bark is more likely to stay attached if a tree or shrub is felled during winter, when the sap isn't rising as fast as in summer. The more stable the wood, the more likely the bark is to stay attached; I have a number of tight-grained bone-dry shrub stems and branches with the bark still on.

When making a straightforward box from a branch you need to detail the join with a V groove that penetrates past the bark; otherwise the join will be less than satisfactory, with little overhangs or shelves. On forms with wider rims, the bark can be retained, but it will be very weak and likely to sustain damage. You can strengthen such rims made of softer woods by impregnating them with cyanoacrylate adhesive.

Wormy banksia on a huon-pine stem; larger box 3⅛ in. (80mm) in diameter. (Boxes by Kath Bretag. Photo by Michal Kluvanek.)

This simple box with the bark intact seemed too plain on the base, so I added a few grooves to break up the surface. Horizontal scrub; about 2½ in. (60mm) in diameter.

Horizontal scrub (left) 4¾ in. (120mm) in diameter. (Box by Simon Raffan.) The plagiarized version (right) would be better without the foot.

Saturn Boxes

Often wide rims occur because of some hairline split you failed to spot in the original blank. As you cut away wood in the search for solid material that you can use, the diameter of the box is reduced. You might consider making a tiny box from the dwindling cylinder, but wide rims are another prospect. And from the idea of wide rims, it is a short step to forms inspired by the planet Saturn (see the top photo below) or other rims that retain the squareness of the blank. (Squared rims can be safely made using waste blocks as in the photos on p. 128.)

For a Saturn-like box, make the rim wide for greater visual impact. Thinner rims would be more effective visually but very fragile given the grain direction. Test the strength of any wood you consider using for such a box by cutting a thin slice of end grain and trying to break it. Some of the acacias are very strong, as are boxwood and African blackwood, allowing you to work very thin. When you make these boxes with threaded lids the ring must be on the lid: If it's on the base you can't cut the male thread.

Planet Spheres, 1984; huon pine; 3 in. (75mm) in diameter. (Boxes by Stephen Hughes.)

Sculptured Profiles

In the mid to late '70s, I made a number of sculptured boxes that had turned insides within a carved profile. For such a profile, the square blanks are held in a chuck while the inside is turned, then the squared outside is carved off the lathe. We tend to think of carving as involving chisels and mallets, but the profiles in the

Saturn Box, 1996; boxwood. The rim is separated from the base but cannot be removed, only spun. (See the drawing on the facing page.) (Box by Hans Weissflog.)

A LOOSE-RING SATURN BOX

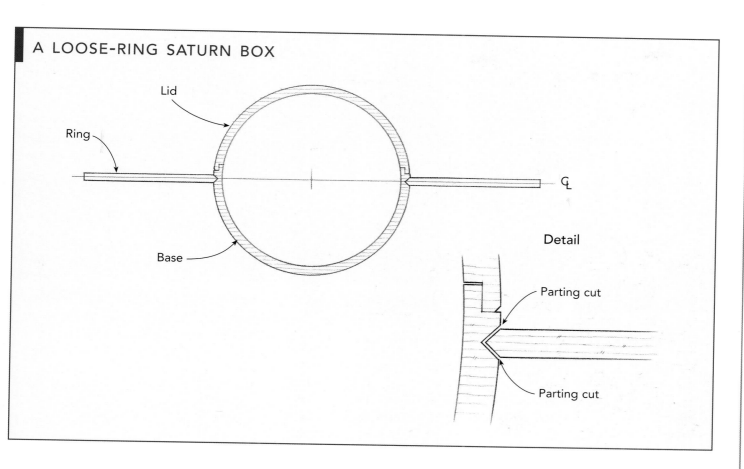

Lid

Ring

Base

C_L

Detail

Parting cut

Parting cut

photo at right were shaped using abrasives, starting with 36 grit. With this technique, the sculptural possibilities are almost endless.

The techniques for making sculptured-profile boxes (see the photos on pp. 126–127) are run-of-the-mill except for the join, where the lid rim and base shoulder must be absolutely flat if the two sections are to meet after you have worked the profile. Thus after you have turned the inside of the lid within the squared blank, turn the rim at 90° to the axis.

If you find turning square sections of these profiles too intimidating—it's easy to catch your knuckles or fingers on the corners—it is safer, although much slower, to use waste blocks as Vic Wood, who is well known for his square-

Sculptured boxes with turned insides, 1997. In the jarrah box (right), I like the curved planes of the sides and the way the top surface sweeps through the join on one corner. Casuarina (left) and jarrah (right); 4 in. (100mm) square.

SATURN BOX

1 Prepare the blank as a cylinder with a ring on. Note that the blank is not set right back into the jaws so that later I can get my finger into the gap.

2 Having parted off the base section, mark the diameter of the cylinder on the face so you don't inadvertently end up with a ring.

3 True the rim face. If you do not go gently, the vibration will scream at you to do so. You might even want to retain the chatter work. If not, support the back of the cut by bringing your finger to the headstock side of the rim.

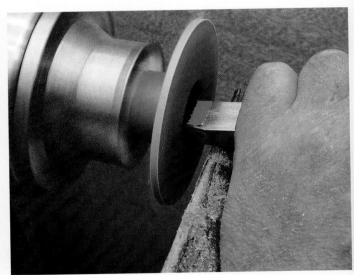

4 Hollowing proceeds as usual. The tape shows the depth required for the hollow. For a sphere, the depth equals half the diameter of the opening.

5 Once the lid is finished and mounted on the base, you have little space in which to operate the skew chisel. I rough the form using a small gouge.

6 For final shaping, I use the skew chisel flat as a scraper, exerting as little pressure as possible against the wood to avoid a catch and torn grain. Near center, at the top of the lid, I have the long point to the right. To get in to the corner where the lid curves into the rim, the long point is to the left.

7 When it comes to finishing the base, rather than turn all the waste away while the base is on a jam chuck, I ease the base to the end of the chuck jaws so I can remove as much as possible while the job is gripped firmly, then reverse chuck to complete the job.

Saturn Boxes about 2½ in. (65mm) in diameter.

SCULPTURED PROFILE BOX

1 The rim must be flat and 90° to the axis. Use a ¾-in. (20mm) square-end scraper with a slightly curved edge. Note how my hand is tight against the rest and around the tool blade. You gain very fine control of the cutting depth by squeezing back with the left hand as the right hand eases the tool forward. By having the tool edge slightly curved, you can use only a small portion at one time and reduce the likelihood of a catch.

2 Check that the rim is flat using a straightedge, not just on the length of the side but also from corner to corner. As usual, the aim is to keep sanding to a minimum on fitting parts like this broad rim.

3 The best way to keep the surface flat is to use a sanding block. Safer but slower is to sand with the lathe off, since you won't have to contend with the corners whizzing around trying to catch your fingers.

4 For the finishing cuts when squaring off the base shoulder, I use a ¾-in. (20mm) skew chisel as a scraper because it allows me to get into the corner more accurately. I could use a skewed scraper, but I have never gotten around to grinding one for this one job.

5 On occasions when you need to sand square sections with the lathe running, wrap the abrasive around a stiff but flexible strip, like a metal rule, which you can bend clear of the oncoming wood. Again, check carefully that the shoulder is flat using a straightedge.

6 Coarse abrasives are a quick and safe way of altering the squared profile. I carve the surfaces using a 36-grit abrasive disk running at 3,500 rpm, with the sides not being sanded taped together to ensure the lid and base stay aligned.

End-grain square boxes. I like the way a lid can be swiveled to break up the series of facets. Casuarina; 2¾ in. (70mm) square. (Boxes by Vic Wood, Melbourne, Australia.)

To make a square-edged form safely, Vic Wood starts with pine scraps glued around the square wood blanks.

The square form is then turned into a cylinder and parted into separate blanks, which are turned as discussed in chapter 4 once the initial turning is complete.

edged forms, does (see the top left photo above). To make sanding easier, to preserve the crisp corners his designs demand, and because it is safer overall, Wood starts with pine waste blocks glued to the basic square blank (see the top right photo above). This piece is then turned to a cylinder and parted into three blanks for separate boxes (see the center and bottom photos at left). Once the turning is complete, the pine is cut away, and the square's faces are sanded and finished.

Roll-Around Forms

I love making boxes that do not have flat bases because they feel so good in the hand. However, they tend to roll about and wobble, especially when they're empty, so I keep them in clutches in a bowl. (Bowls for rounded forms represent a sales opportunity for those of you doing a bit of marketing.)

The fit of the lid is crucial on any form that rests on its side because there is not much gravity to keep the lid in place. Loose lids will not stay on, so you need to have a really snug fit or to cut threads.

The black gidgee lid on the small acorn is too heavy for the huon-pine base, so the box only sits properly when containing enough weight to counterbalance the lid. A heavy diamond would be ideal. 3 in., 2⅜ in., and 1¾ in. (75mm, 60mm, and 45mm) in diameter.

I love making boxes that do not have flat bases because they feel so good in the hand.

Rounded forms are best kept in a bowl so they cannot roll too far.

Seed pod with screw top; casuarina; 3 in. (90mm) in diameter.

Egg boxes. In this clutch, the jacaranda (right), with too full a curve on the pointy end, is barely egg shaped but still passable from an avian standpoint. From left to right: alder, cherry, African blackwood, jacaranda; 3¾ in. (95mm) to 2½ in. (65mm) in diameter.

On most forms it is immediately apparent which end is the lid. But making this distinction obvious is generally a good idea anyway because you are less likely to spill the contents upon opening the box. Aesthetically, these forms look better if the lid end sits higher than the base, so how you distribute weight in the box wall becomes crucial to achieving a good balance: The weight needs to be in the base.

Of all the rounded forms that can be turned, eggs are probably the most popular. They are also a challenge because it is not easy to keep the curve flowing so you get a form that could pass from a bird without killing it (see the bottom left photo on p. 129).

Another variation of the rounded form is the seed pod (see the bottom right photo on p. 129). It's the same basic shape as an egg, but it comes to a point at one end and can have a finial on the lid for decoration. Here the lid screws on, and the tail is carved on a sanding disk to be slightly curled. To create the hint of a curl on the tail, the form is turned with a flared end, which is then carved away to leave an off-center point. To keep the lid pitched up, the tail is left solid (see the drawing at left). The combination of weight and carving in the tail means the form can roll only so far. An alternative solution to curb a rolling box is a stand (see the photos below).

Miniatures

Miniatures are fun to do so you can say you've been there and done that (see the left photo on the facing page). Perhaps surprisingly, the biggest problem in making miniatures is not being unable to see what you're doing but rather fitting the lids. (If your eyesight begins to let you down, as mine does, try some model-

SEED-POD BOX

Keep some mass in the tail so the lid is pitched up when the box sits on a flat surface.

$\mathfrak{C}_L$

Portion carved away

To curb a rolling box you can use a stand. This stand was turned as a wide ring, then carved using a drum sander with 36-, 60-, 120-, and 240-grit abrasives. Laburnum; 2⅜ in. (60mm) in diameter.

maker's magnifying lenses. I have a x3 magnification set that clips on my glasses, and I can see everything I want.) Fitting lids on very small diameters is difficult because of the very small margin for error. The work is done the same way as discussed in chapter 4, but you need much more finesse on this small scale.

It pays to vacuum the area around the lathe so that if the lid comes off you have some hope of finding it. Don't use a dust extractor while you're turning in case a lid flies in. But the biggest challenge is usually that, having made a minuscule lid, you have to hollow an even more minuscule base. You can make tiny tools from nails for hollowing, but drills are an easier way to go; you can use a ½-in. (15mm) skew chisel for the profile.

Miniatures; huon pine; the smallest is ³⁄₁₆ in. (5mm) in diameter.

Pod Boxes

These c. 3-in.- (75mm) diameter Pod boxes are inspired by eucalyptus seed pods. The flared top is mostly carved away to create the asymmetry.

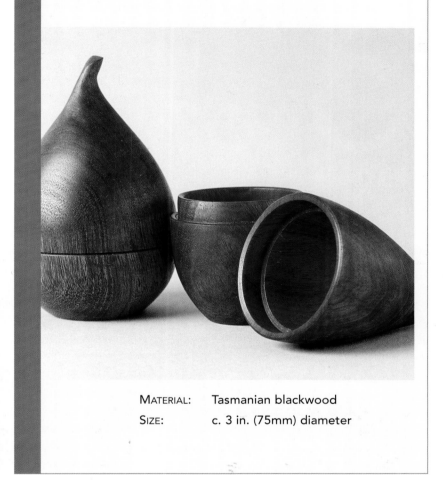

MATERIAL:	Tasmanian blackwood
SIZE:	c. 3 in. (75mm) diameter

Fitting lids on very small diameters is difficult because of the very small margin for error.

Drill containers; Tasmanian blackwood; 10⅞ in. (275mm) and 6⅛ in. (155mm) tall.

Earring containers. To save wood otherwise lost in the long overlap, the center column in the laburnum box (right) is a preturned cocobolo cylinder glued in place with cyanoacrylate adhesive. Casuarina (left) and laburnum and cocobolo (right); 3⅜ in. (85mm) and 2¾ in. (70mm) in diameter, respectively. (Dolphin earrings by Beth Arbuckle, Bountiful, Utah.)

To balance the form on the laburnum box (right in the photo above), I added a band of decoration. The V grooves were shear cut using the long point of the skew chisel, then rounded somewhat by abrasives.

Likewise, the join line of the casuarina box (left in the bottom left photo) looked better after I added lines to link it more to the lid (photo above right).

Experimenting should be fun, and if you pull off a masterpiece or merely enhance your previously lackluster forms, that is a bonus.

Drill Containers

This type of box makes a good excursion into deep hollowing (see the top left photo on the facing page). Make as tall a lid as you can, then fit it over a solid base into which you drill holes using a pillar drill. I begin really deep holes on the pillar drill but complete them using a hand drill so I can wiggle the drill around to enlarge the hole enough for the drills being stored to drop in easily.

Earring Containers

Earring containers are great to make as a special gift (see the top right photo on the facing page). The lids need to be loose so they can be removed using one hand. Anyone who wears earrings would be pleased to have several of these boxes.

Needle Cases

Sewing needles come in a variety of shapes and sizes, but they are rarely very long or large, so the boxes to contain them hardly ever exceed 4 in. (100mm) in length. A good fit is essential, so keep the flanges long.

A needle case's small diameter and comparative length make the inside very difficult to hand-turn, so it is commonly drilled out. I do not bother to turn my squared blanks to round, but instead pop them straight into the chuck for drilling. This is partly for speed and partly to retain the bulk of material during the drilling process in case the wood feels like splitting.

Needle cases; kingwood (dark boxes in rear) and celery top pine (front); about 4 in. (100mm) long.

Experiments

We all make things from time to time that are less than satisfactory, often missing our original intentions by a country mile. And there are the more frequent "just-misses," which need that little extra something. These are the pieces to play around with, possibly working with other turners or makers from other disciplines to

NEEDLE CASE

1 These four blanks have the parts identified. The drills are used for hollowing each section.

2 If you have only standard jaws for your chuck, remove them for such small jobs as this and grip the square using the slides.

3 Mount the lid blank top into the jaws, and true the end grain, leaving an inward chamfer on the rim as usual.

4 Drill the lid. The tape marks the required depth. The drill, mounted in the tail center, should leave a near-perfect surface ready for polishing.

5 Mount the base section with the bottom outward, and true to a cylinder.

6 Reverse the base section and drill out the center. For production, grind a depth mark on the drill, seen in the photo midway between the wood and the chuck.

7 Cut the base flange to fit the lid. Once the diameter is established, turn a flange at least ¾ in. (20mm) long.

8 Turn the lid. When turning the end it pays to use your hand to support the work as cutting proceeds. Remember your hand is there to equalize the pressure of the tool: If your hand gets too hot, you are pushing the tool too hard into the wood. Note how the ⅜-in. (10mm) gouge is pressed firmly against my thumb, while my forefinger is wrapped around the job.

9 Rechuck the base using the drill as a mandrill or jam chuck. Because of twisting grain, I make a peeling/scrape cut, using my thumb to keep the tool on the rest and my fingers to equalize the pressure of the cut.

10 When the base is remounted there is usually some eccentricity, which in this photo can be seen between the darker polished surface and the paler, newly turned surfaces. These eccentricities vanish with 240-grit abrasives, which blend the two surfaces.

This box was charred, then the surface was brushed before the brass escutcheon pins were glued into predrilled holes. (Box decorated by Terry Baker.)

Here the textured surfaces were charred and softened to highlight the striations beneath the gold leaf. (Box decorated by Terry Baker.)

A box with a lid that's difficult to remove if it jams is a prime candidate for experimentation. Casuarina; 3 in. (75mm) in diameter.

Here the surface was carved before nails were inserted. (Box decorated by Terry Baker.)

bounce ideas off one another, not worrying if you make a complete mess of things.

It is the playing around and experimenting that is important here—the journey, not the arrival. Experimenting should be fun, and if you pull off a masterpiece or merely enhance your previously lackluster forms, that is a bonus. In the background there's the possibility of some insight that can send you off in a different direction.

In one of my experiments, I made boxes with the idea of having interchangeable lids so that the forms could be altered when we felt in need of a change. In one case, the lid clearly needed extra work, so I packed it off with a few other boxes to Terry Baker, an artist, ceramicist, and turner friend living just north of Sydney whose special interest is surfaces. We have worked together several times, and writing this book offered another excuse. In the top photos on the facing page, we can see how his simple patterns snapped my forms into life.

In the top left photo on the facing page, Baker turned away the point on the lid and charred the brushed profile using a blowtorch before inserting the brass escutcheon pins. The pins are glued into holes with cyanoacrylate adhesive, rather than driven home, which would damage the domed heads and reduce their luster. The holes are not laid out on a rigid grid but drilled by eye, which is more in keeping with the coarse textures of the base and lends a more spontaneous feel to the whole box.

In the top right photo on the facing page, Baker charred and softened my textured surfaces somewhat to highlight his striations beneath the gold-colored leaf, which really shines out from the dark matte surface.

All angles and no practicality, a conical lid is really difficult to remove if it jams, so it is a prime candidate for experimentation. I had intended to carve the conical lid in the bottom left photo on the facing page, but Baker decided on a wilder approach, carving the surface before

I rounded over the flat bottom of this box so that now it appears to be the lid. Cocobolo; 1⅜ in. (35mm) in diameter.

inserting nails of patinated copper (see the bottom right photo on the facing page). The flatheads were crimped so that when set at angles they provide differing patterns when viewed from various angles.

If you are not satisfied with your efforts and have the wall thickness to play with, do something. The piece in the bottom photo above looked like a lost carrot, so I rounded over the flat bottom, detailing it so it looks to be the lid (see the top photo above).

9 FORMS

The aim of this chapter is to present groups of shapes that provide a platform from which you can develop your own variations. These shapes are not offered as perfect forms, although I am very pleased with many of them. If you want to replicate any shapes exactly, photocopy them and make a template by cutting out the profile. You might find it a useful exercise, but I think a better way to use these shapes is to allow them to trigger an I-might-try-one-of-those response, then close the book and get to it. Don't forget the option of turning a solid form in waste timber to see if your tools and techniques work with my designs. If they don't,

you are on the way to putting your own stamp on what you make.

People have often shown me "copies" of the boxes in my first book, frequently being most apologetic. Some have been good, some bad, and others appalling, but I never cease to be amazed at the diversity of shapes emerging from that common source. But then when did parents spawn clones of themselves, be they animal or plant. Nature obviously considers it undesirable, and so do I.

The solid black forms in this section were all turned using only a ¾-in. (20mm) skew chisel, a ⅜-in. (10mm) shallow gouge, and a parting tool.

The way to use these shapes is to allow them to trigger an I-might-try-one-of-those response, then close the book and get to it.

Standing forms look better when the curves and finial on the lid lead the eye upward.

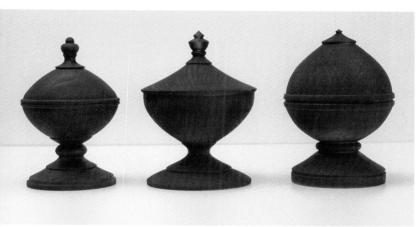

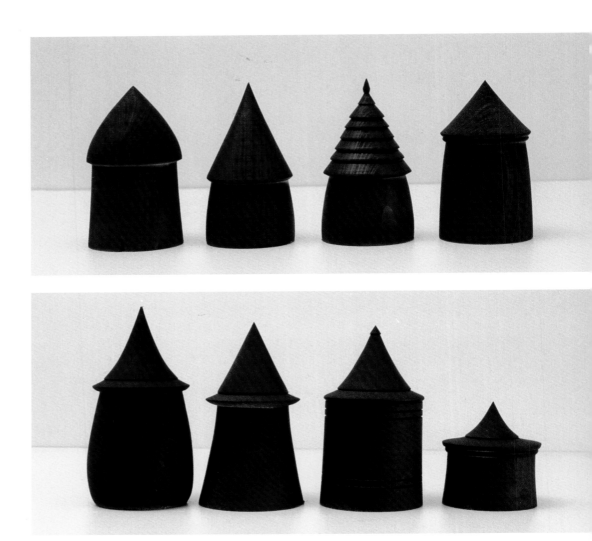

These forms are based on medieval European buildings.

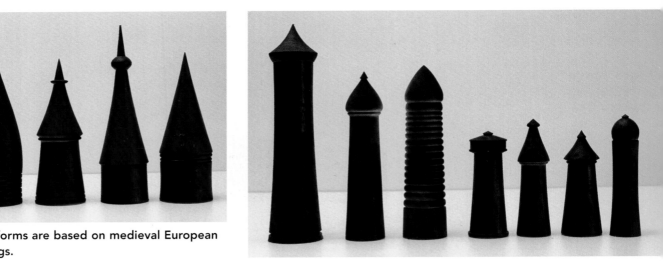

To avoid straight lines, these boxes are slightly curved and asymmetric.

Lids can be difficult to remove, so ensure that the rim overhangs the base or incorporates a concave curve you can grip.

Rounded forms are not suited to tight-fitting lids because the profiles are too difficult to grasp. Go for the merest hint of suction so that as you raise the lid the base is barely lifted by the suction.

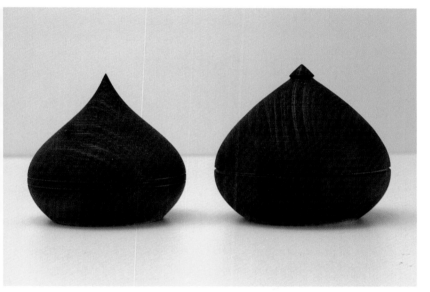

Mushroom forms often look better if you can keep the bark. (Boxes at center and below by Jim Stevenson.)

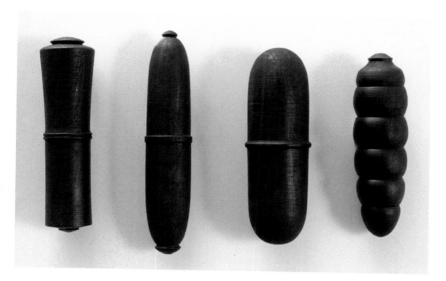

These forms are ideal for pocket boxes. Since they can roll around, threaded lids are preferable. (Cow Horn Acorn Box and Acorn Box at bottom left by Bonnie Klein.)

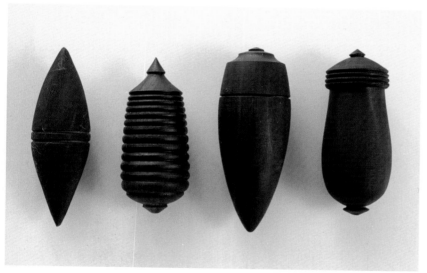

CHAPTER

10 FINISHING

My finishing kit includes a turned box for the current oil rag, a lump of beeswax, and a clean rag. The scrubbing brush is used to buff textured surfaces.

One dent or stain might look like a disaster, whereas a thousand marks and regular polishing make a patina.

To finish your boxes, a host of manufacturers have thoughtfully provided a vast array of oils, waxes, polishes, lacquers, and synthetic products—all of which aim to bring out the color and natural beauty of the wood while minimizing the need for ongoing attention. The emphasis of these products is on speed and ease of application and on longevity of the finish, but I generally get the finish I want on my boxes in a few seconds using a lump of pure beeswax, a bit of rag, and occasionally some oil.

Finishing is not the preoccupation for me that it is for so many woodworkers, but a vast amount is published in books and magazines by specialists in the art, and it is to them I would refer you for detailed information, particularly if you want a high-gloss finish.

I dislike hard and shiny finishes, belonging to the school that considers that the plastic look is too artificial and detracts from the natural material beneath. Observation tells me that wood sealed with a hard finish will look fine for a few years until the finish starts to show signs of wear and tear or crack up, after which it generally looks unattractive. Then the temptation is to discard the box for looking too tatty rather

These boxes are well battered from years of use containing screws in the workshop, but their patina is building nicely. 2⅜ in. (60mm) in diameter.

than refinish it because refinishing is too difficult if you have no lathe or finishing expertise.

I make boxes in the hope they will be used and treasured for generations, and consequently I use a softer beeswax or oil finish that is unaffected by small dents and scratches. A beeswax and oil finish never chips, unlike a harder finish. I know that if my boxes are used and handled regularly, each will soon develop the sort of patina associated with well-used tool handles or furniture (see the photo above). It is the combination of all the knocks of daily life overlaid with polish imparted through dust and sweaty hands that creates the lustrous surfaces universally admired on well-used wooden objects.

You can take too much care of wood, never using it in case of accidents and never polishing it in case you ruin the surface. But take the risk: One dent or stain might look like a disaster, whereas a thousand marks and regular polishing make a patina. For a really deep luster, you cannot beat regular polishing to maintain a finish, following the old rule of thumb: every day for a month, every week for a year, and every month thereafter.

The density of the wood dictates whether or not you need to use oil. The more open-grained

Domed Boxes

The beads at the join disguise the fact that the grain doesn't quite match, and the satin finish provides a soft luster that helps the surfaces flow together.

MATERIALS: Cherry (left), cocobolo (right)
SIZES: Left: 3⅛ in. by 6⅞ in. (80mm by 175mm) and right: 1⅞ in. by 2⅜ in. (47mm by 60mm)

Tower Series Boxes

A tall box is easier to make if the lid is threaded. The right-hand box has two small storage areas, unscrewing at the beaded sections.

MATERIAL: Tasmanian blackwood
SIZES: 2 in. (50mm) diameter

Top: Wax alone failed to finish the end grain of this cocobolo piece satisfactorily, leaving a number of pores unfilled that show as white dots. Bottom: Oil has been applied, then another layer of wax, and the dots are gone.

woods with large pores will look better if soaked in oil before any wax is applied; otherwise the end grain remains a mass of little white dots (see the photos above). In general, oils are used to penetrate the wood and bring out the color and grain, while waxes are used to seal the surface.

However, on most timbers I use a lump of plain beeswax to get the soft luster I want. Although beeswax is readily available from woodturning supply stores, if you live in the country, you might be able to get it direct from a friendly apiarist. Recently I was given a big bucket of beehive tailings in which wax was mixed in with assorted bits of bee, honey, and general beehive muck. I had a lovely time messing up the kitchen while melting the wax into small cartons and generally splashing it around. As it cooled, the scum and everything I didn't want rose to the top, so I scraped this off and retained the pure wax below. I now have enough to last decades, and although I enjoyed the experience, it is a lot easier and a lot less messy to buy beeswax in blocks from a store.

To apply the beeswax, hold a lump against the wood as it spins on the lathe and build up a visible layer. Then take a soft lint-free rag and push this hard against the wax and wood so the wax melts with the friction and can be flowed into every corner with the rag. Never wrap the rag around your fingers in case it gets caught by the lathe. The heat lets some of the wax penetrate the wood, but most wax will be absorbed by the rag, which soon becomes so impregnated with wax that all you need to do is apply the rag to shine up a surface and bring out the color of the wood.

Mostly I use this very simple, quick, and effective method of finishing, but if straight wax leaves the end grain looking as though it needs a bit more attention, I wipe on thin oil then rewax over the top. In the past I have used cooking oil or mineral oil, although these days I am experimenting with some of the new thin penetrating oils and very soft commercial waxes. I always ensure these are nontoxic in case the boxes are used in the kitchen or for food, sweets, lollies, or candy.

When turning more open-grained timbers, I use my standard universal finish for bowls, spindles, and boxes, which is similar to that described previously. Using a soft cloth, I slosh oil liberally over the wood with the lathe off, then start the lathe and melt on a thin but visible layer of wax before applying the rag. By holding the rag firmly against the surface you blend the oil and wax, with the bulk absorbed into the rag, which becomes so saturated that, like the wax-impregnated rag mentioned earlier, it can be used without applying oil separately. However, when a rag gets to a condition when it leaves the surface slightly oily, you need a cleaner, drier cloth for a final rub. I have a number of rags in use ranging from clean to filthy,

Never wrap the rag around your fingers in case it gets caught by the lathe.

Oil and beeswax give a low sheen. Of these boxes only the one at the front left is new; the others are several years old and are oiled and waxed regularly.

and I move them from one grade to another until they fall apart. The whole finishing operation is very fast, taking only a few seconds to produce a low sheen, but it is not a long-lasting finish and needs maintenance or use or both.

Most of the finishing products available commercially combine oils or waxes (or a combination of oils and waxes) with solvents so the finish can be applied easily then harden as the solvents evaporate. Some harden rapidly during the polishing, while others take more time. The degree of luster, gloss, or brilliance achievable is usually well described on the packet, jar, can, or bottle, and there will be instructions as to application. So, whatever finish you want, there will be many products available to help you achieve it. Or you could stick to the wax and oil, like I do.

AFTERWORD

We never reach perfection: That's what keeps every living thing trying to improve on the status quo. I'm sure that even ancient species successful for millions of years, such as sharks and crocodiles, refine their hunting techniques just as we hone our ability to leave the planet or bake better loaves of bread. When turning a box you will find infinite scope for improvement as you search for the ideal combination of balance and a functioning lid.

Remember that something is good only in relation to something similar. To say that snakes are better than spiders is meaningless, whereas to say that taipans are more beautiful or more deadly than rattlesnakes is valid. By comparing our successes and failures with previous efforts, we can chart our course toward perfection, even if we never get there. It is often better to travel hopefully than to arrive. Enjoy the journey.

Graveyard

If you have no failures, you are not trying.

INDEX

Index note: page references in bold indicate a drawing; page references in italics indicate a photograph.